Teacher Jeanette

GETTING STARTED
with Alphabet & Numbers

a Primer for Beginners

Ophelia S. Lewis

Village Tales Publishing

MINNEAPOLIS, MN

Village Tales Publishing
www.villagetalespublishing.com
www.oass.villagetalespublishing.com
www.villagetalespublishing.com/childrensbooks

Book Cover and formatting by OASS
ISBN: 9781959580003

A Liberia Literary Society
Educational Project

Printed in the USA

This book belongs to:

_____

How to care for your book.

1. Read with clean hands.
2. Turn pages carefully.
3. Keep your book in your bookbag
when you're not reading it.
4. Keep your book close to you
when reading, so that you don't drop it.
5. Use a bookmark
to save your page in a book.
6. Keep your book away
from food and drinks.
7. Only draw, write, and color
where instructed to.
8. Keep your book away
from younger siblings and pets.

Primary Handwriting Guidelines

Sit down and place book flat in front of you.

Use your helper hand to hold the paper down **while writing.**

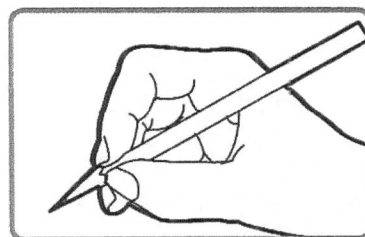

Correctly hold your pencil; only move the fingers when writing.

Notes on the Contributors

Manseen Logan is a Liberian-American editor and writer. She published the first story in the "Adventures at Camp Pootie-Cho" children's book series. In the series, readers can learn about Liberia's endangered wildlife, the unique rainforest, and valuable life lessons. She enjoys participating in kids' book readings sponsored by Liberia Literary Society.

Patrice Juah is a communications professional, writer and editor. As founder of the Martha Juah Educational Foundation, she champions girls' education and leadership, through the foundation's academic initiative, Sexy Like A Book. An accomplished author, poet, and public speaker, her literary works cover a wide range of themes, to include personal life experiences, women's empowerment and humor. A firm believer in the transformative power of education, Juah contributes to the Liberia Literary Society and Village Tales Publishing, as board member and editor, respectively.

Ophelia S. Lewis is the CEO of the Liberia Literary Society organization, which provides resources to preserve Liberia's literary works, advance girls' education and youth development. Giving children a chance to learn is one of the most urgent priorities in Liberia. As a published author and humanitarian, Lewis takes on the dire, yet fulfilling task of giving children an opportunity to start a solid educational journey. Hopefully, the synergy of Liberia Literary Society and Village Tales Publishing will produce effective results for students. Quality education is key to any society's success; this ignites Lewis' passion for writing children's books.

Teacher Jeanette Kinder Kollege workbooks are packed with exercises that will make learning fun! These workbooks will provide a gentle introduction to structured learning that is both developmentally appropriate and academically foundational. They are proven activities to help prepare Liberian students for success; by teaching strong fundamentals to start their educational journey. Students will LOVE learning.

Introduction

The first thing we teach preschoolers is letters and counting because these skills are foundational to all knowledge they'll acquire through the year. However, the first thing we introduce on the first day of school should be 'mindset'. What does mindset mean? To put it simply, mindset is a way of thinking. Before learning the alphabet, introduce the word mindset to your students. Mindset is the way we think. They don't need to understand the importance of their way of thinking, or worldview right now, but you need to show them how to use their brain (think). It will define how they look at the world, approach things, and behave when faced with difficult or unexpected situations. Our mindset influences how we think, feel, and behave in any given situation. It means that what we believe about ourselves impacts our success or failure. The Teacher's Edition has an entire section on how to teach students about mindset.

Pre-Kindergarten is the foundation of a child's education. The educational "house" a child builds in his/her life will be built on the foundation of pre-kindergarten. It is during the first years of life that children form attitudes about themselves, others, learning, and the environment. Educating a child is most successful when teachers and schools work together in the best interest of the child. Valuing education and the opportunities it provides are important first steps.

Teacher Jeanette Kinder Kollege workbooks are packed with exercises that will make learning fun! These workbooks will provide a gentle introduction to structured learning that is both developmentally appropriate and academically foundational. They are proven activities to help prepare Liberian students for success; by teaching strong fundamentals to start their educational journey. Students will LOVE learning.

Contents

TEACHERS PLANT♡ SEEDS THAT GROW FOREVER

THE BRAIN CAN GROW!

I Can!

I can
IMPROVE
if I keep
TRYING

I will not give up!
I know
things can get better!
I know
I can learn new things!

The Alphabet

My Brain is Ready to Grow!

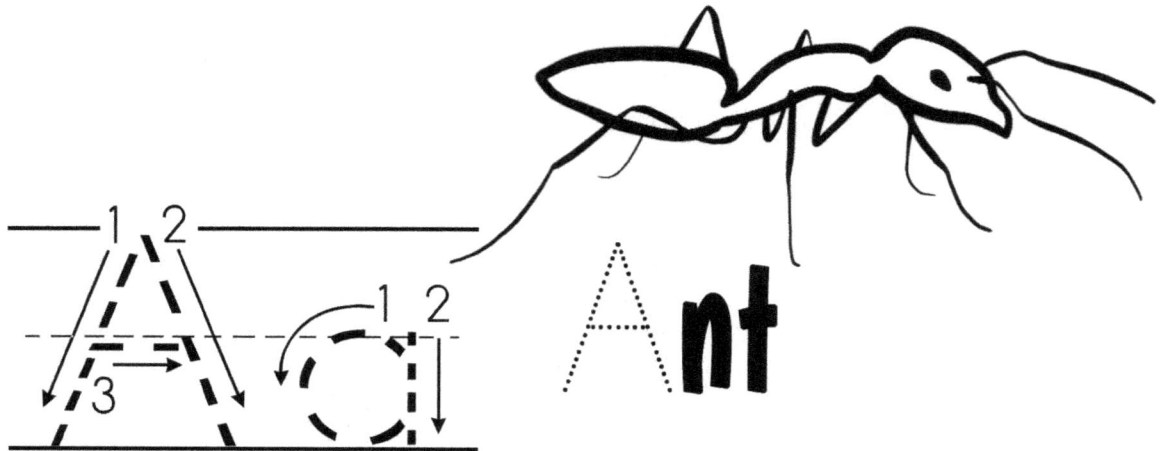

Ant

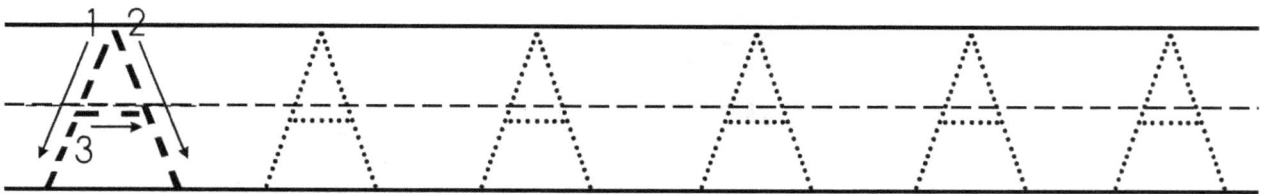

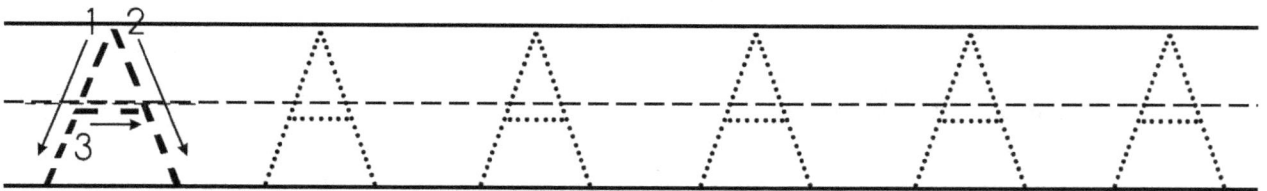

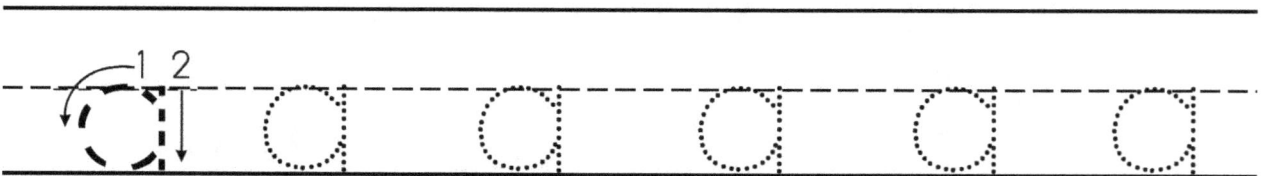

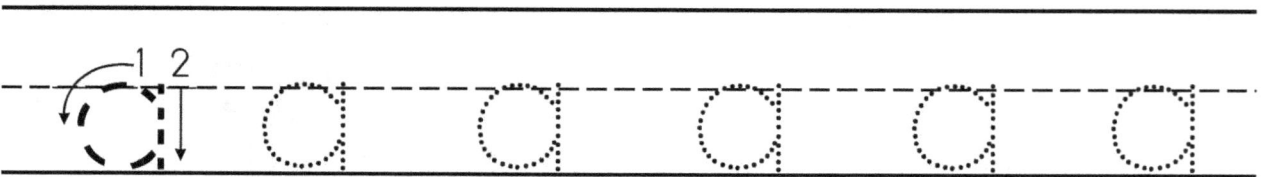

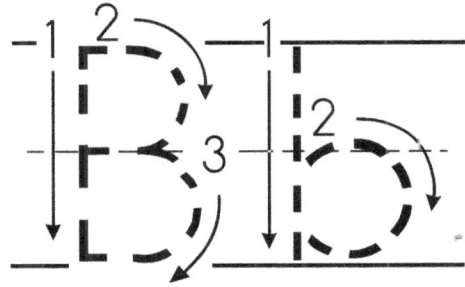

B**ird**

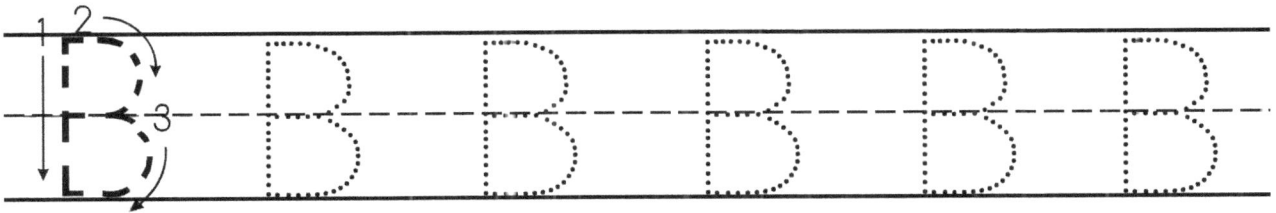

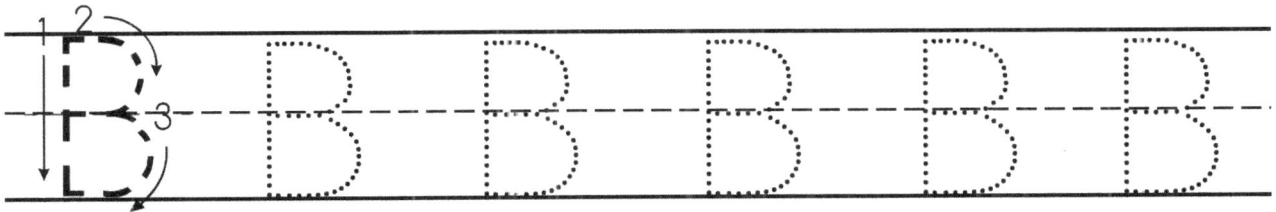

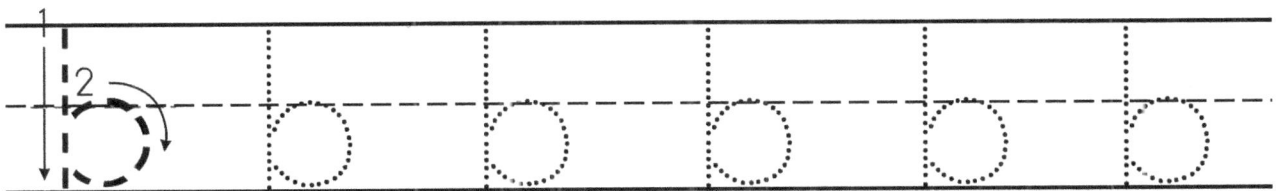

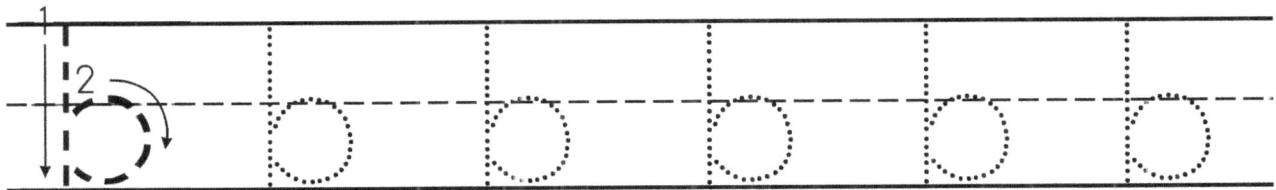

15

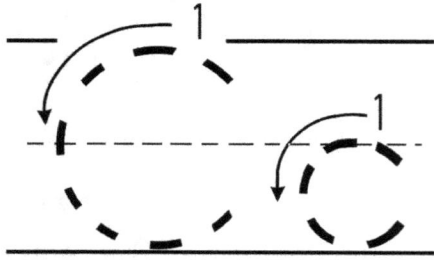

Cow

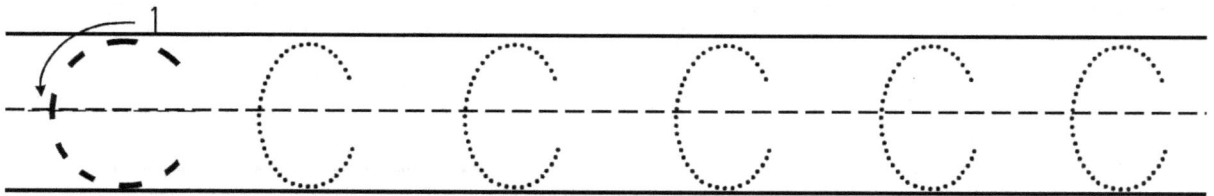

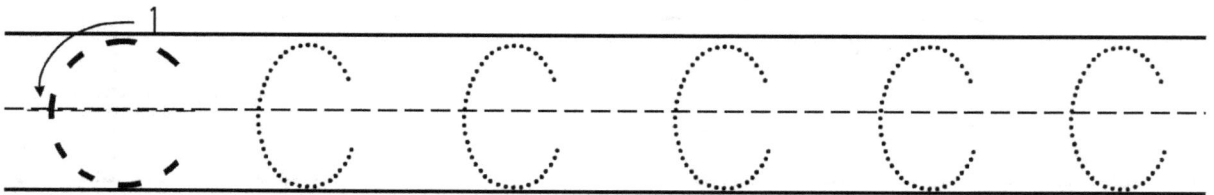

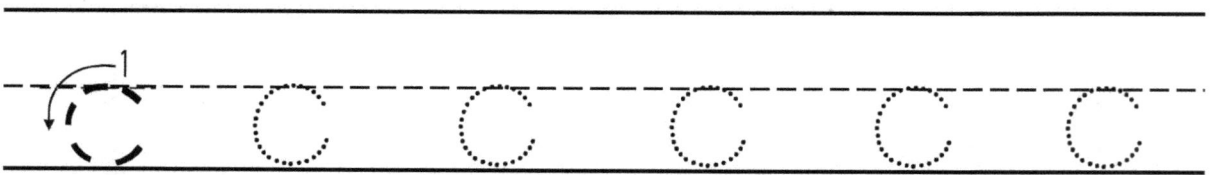

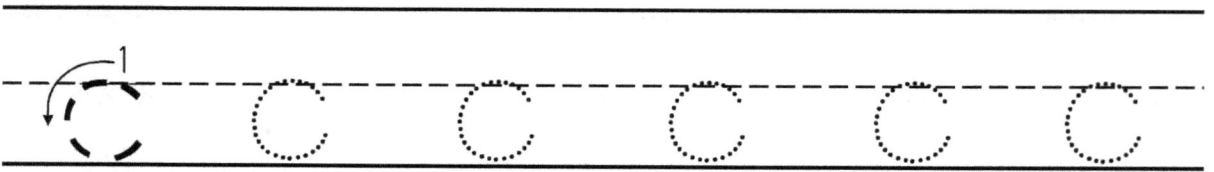

16

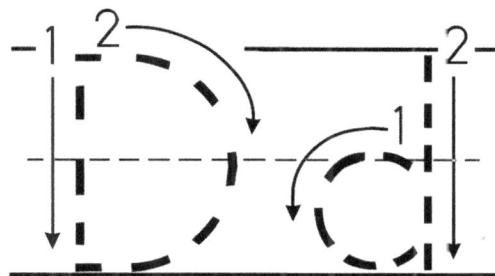

Dog

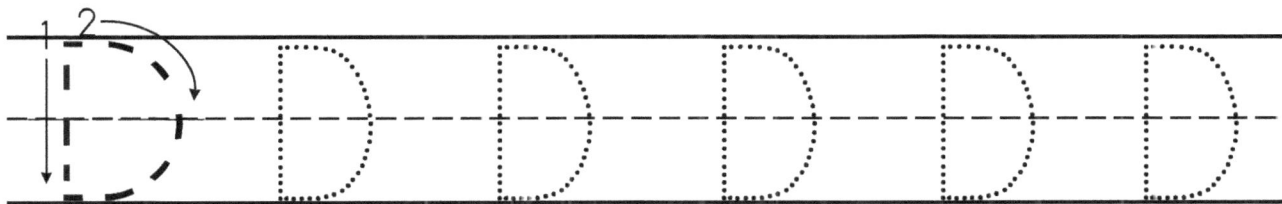

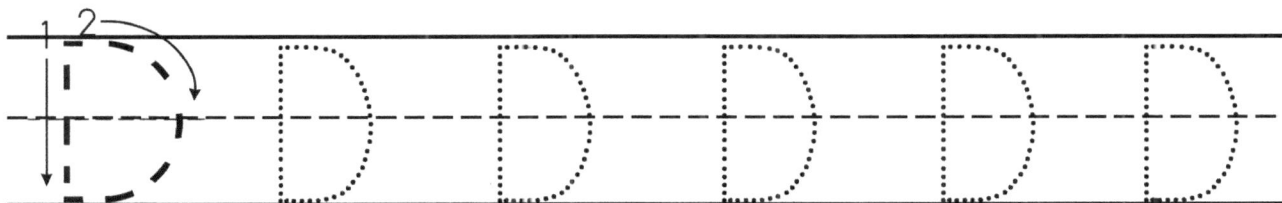

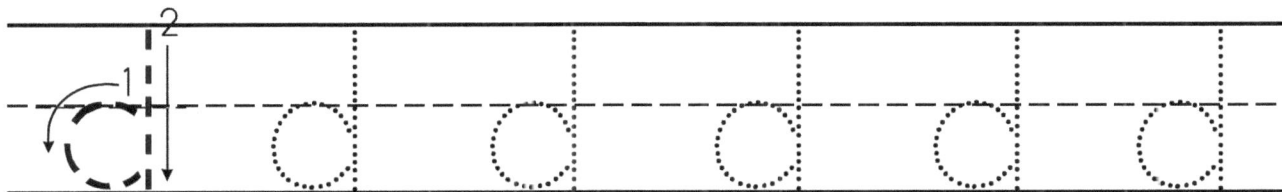

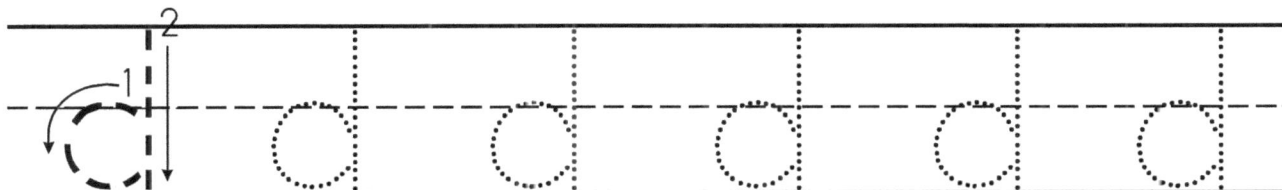

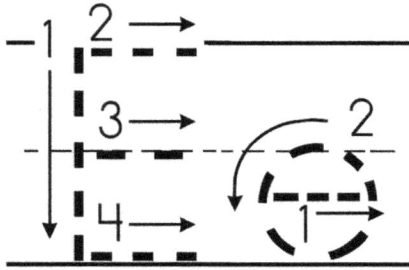

E**gg**

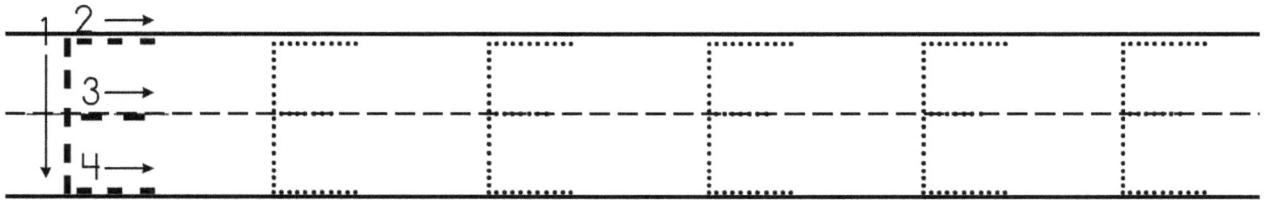

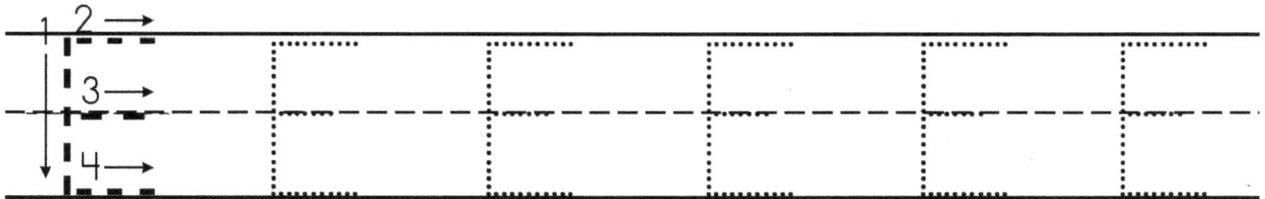

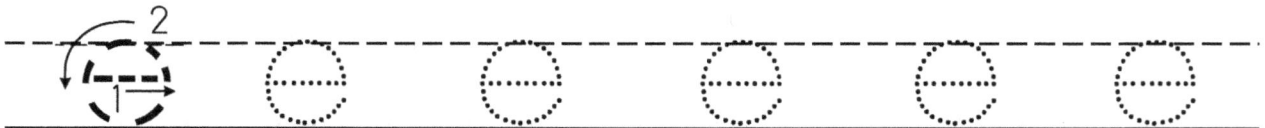

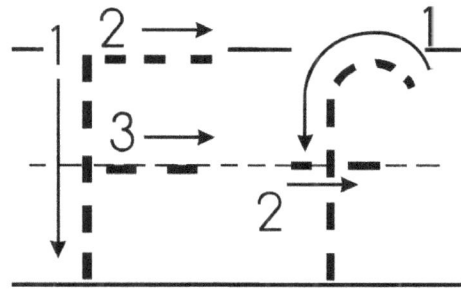

Fish

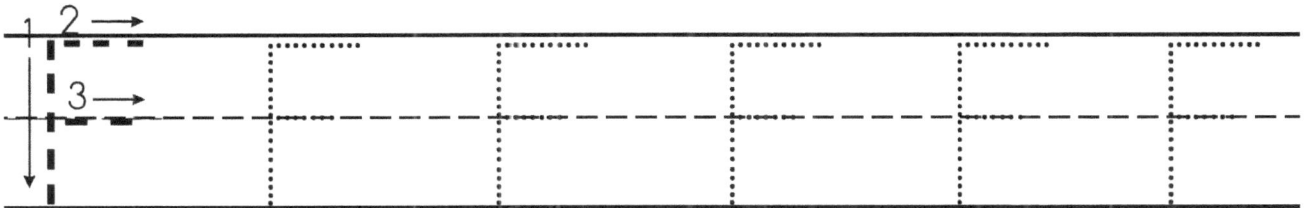

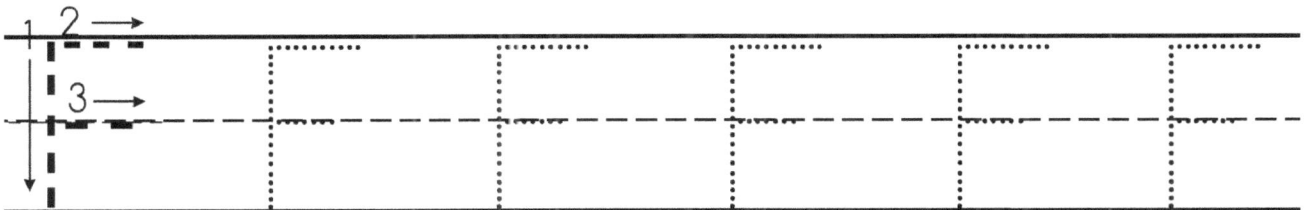

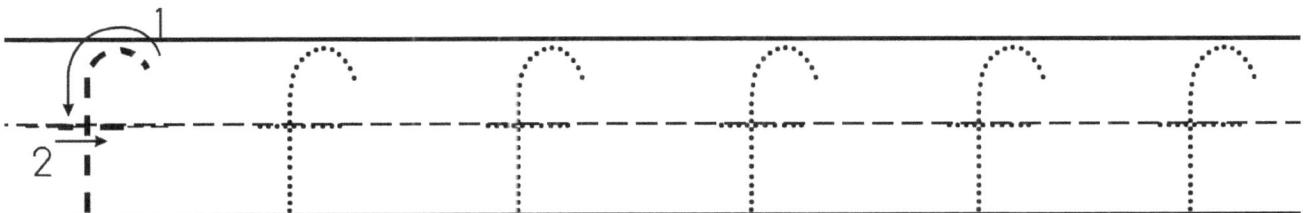

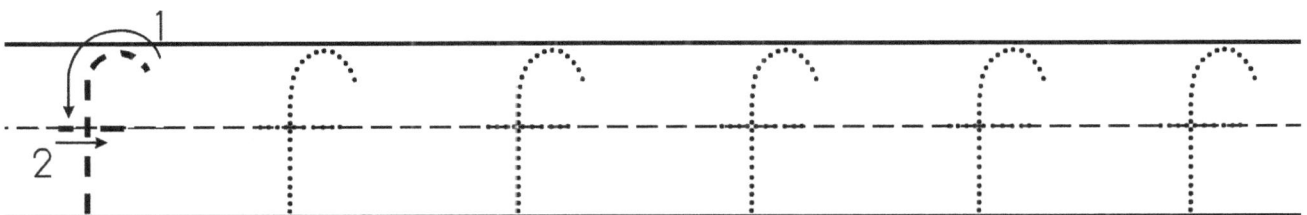

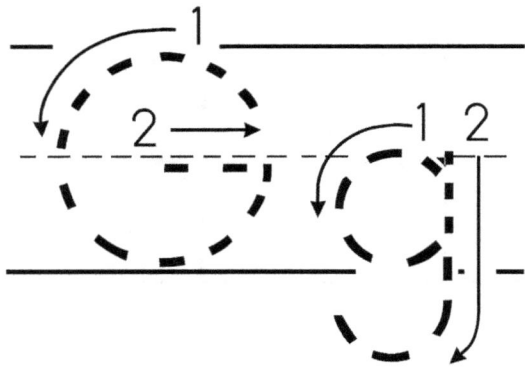

Goat

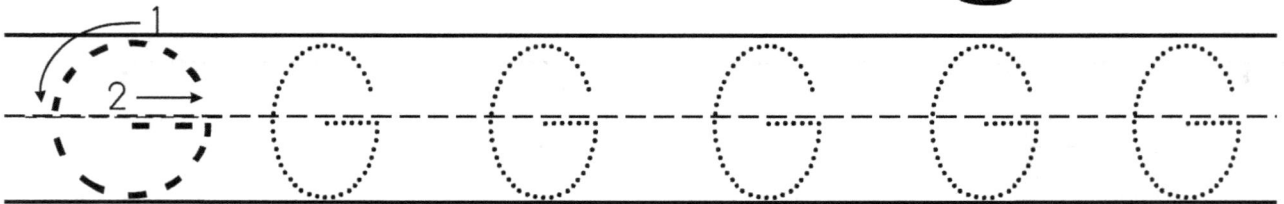

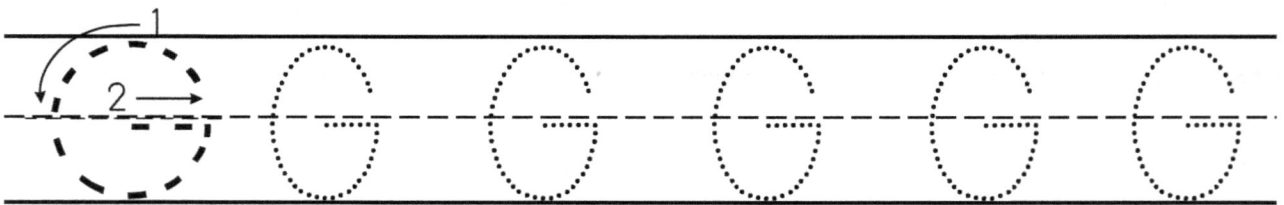

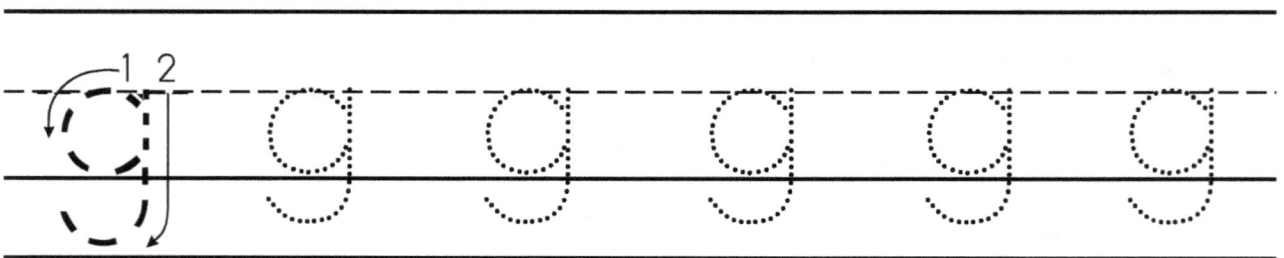

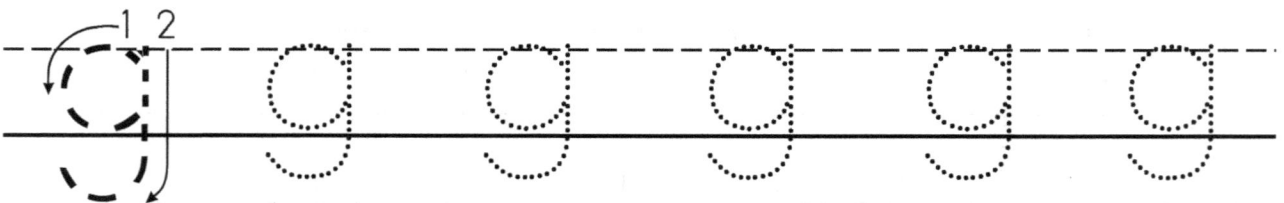

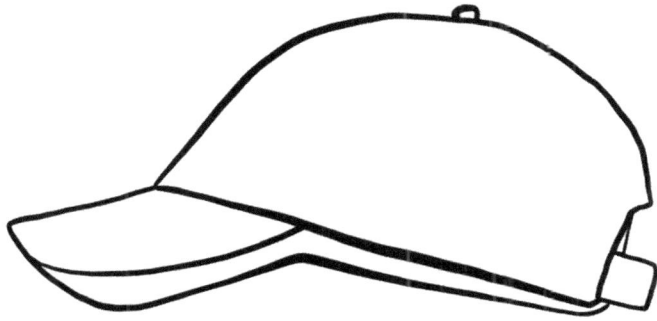

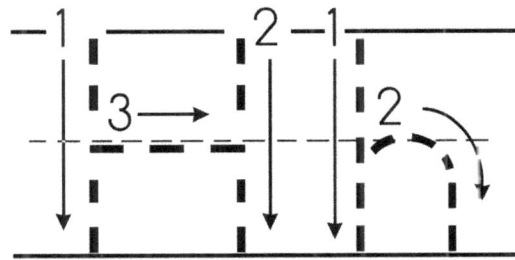

Hat

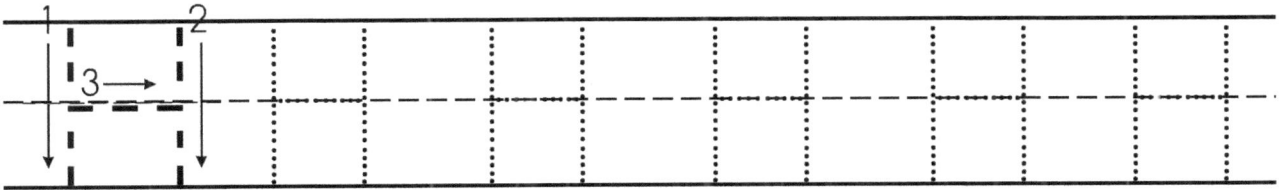

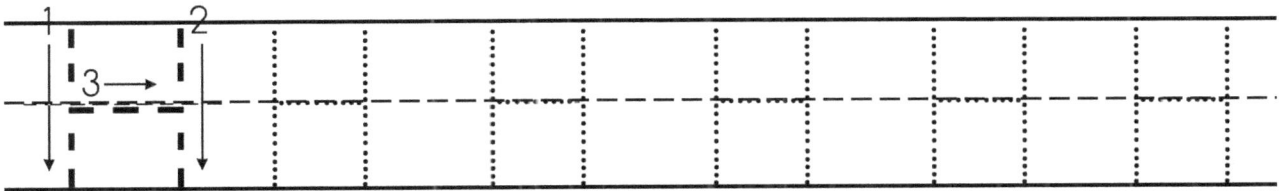

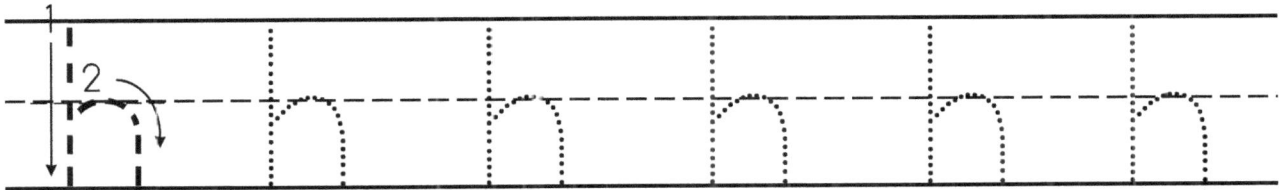

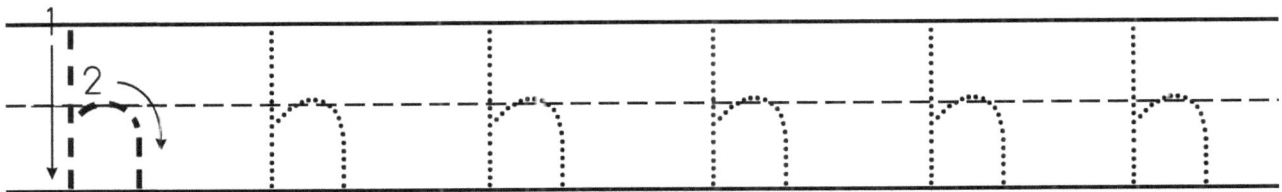

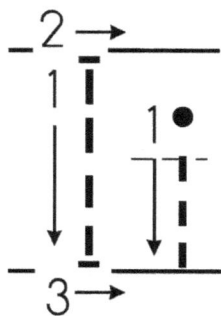

Ice cream

22

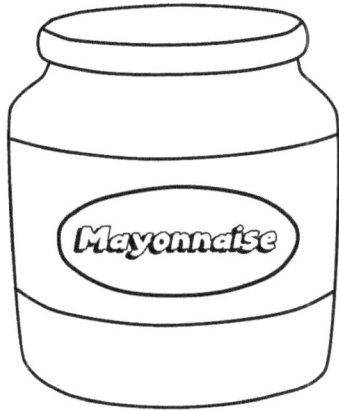

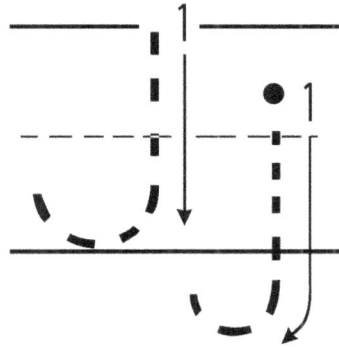

Jar

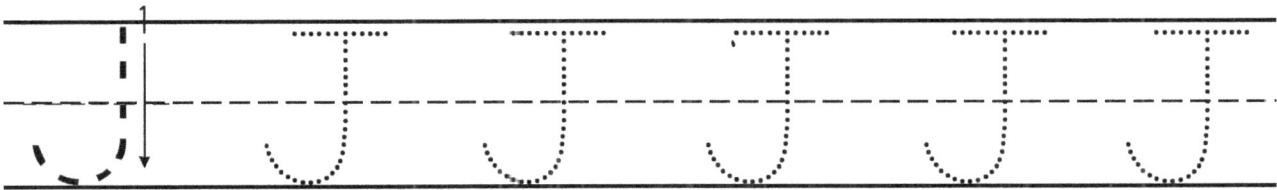

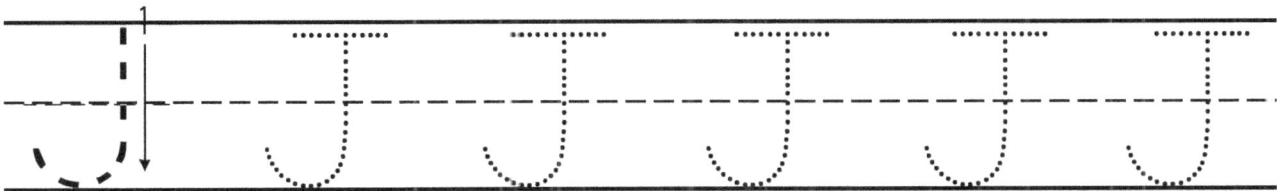

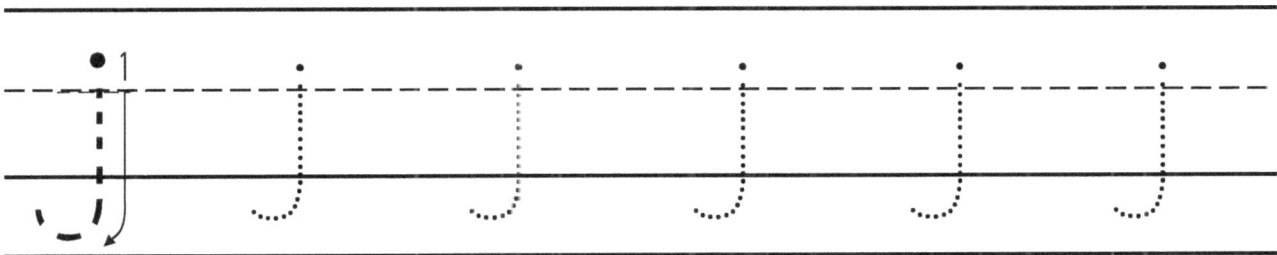

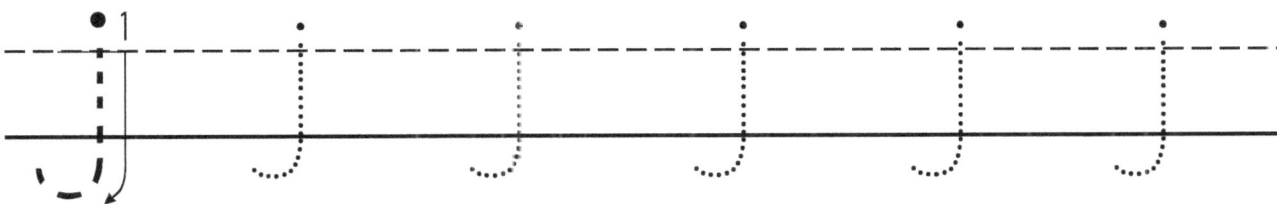

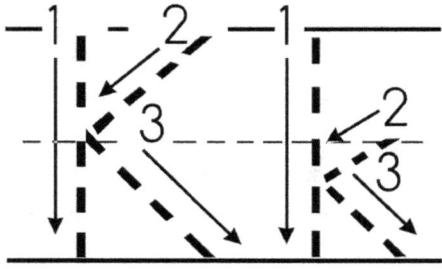

K ey

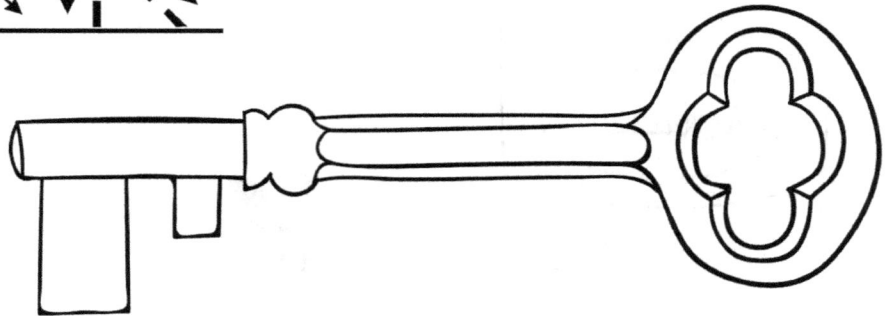

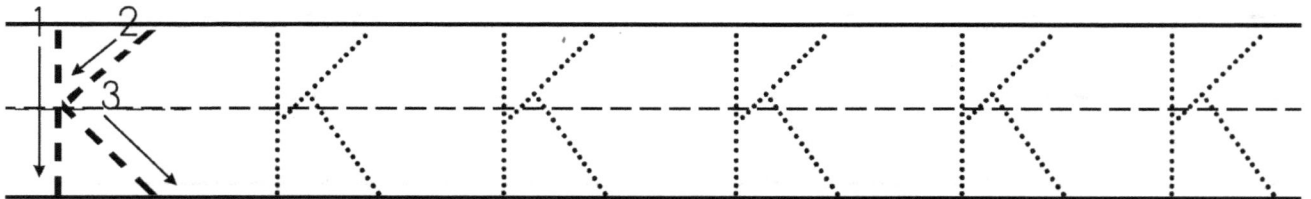

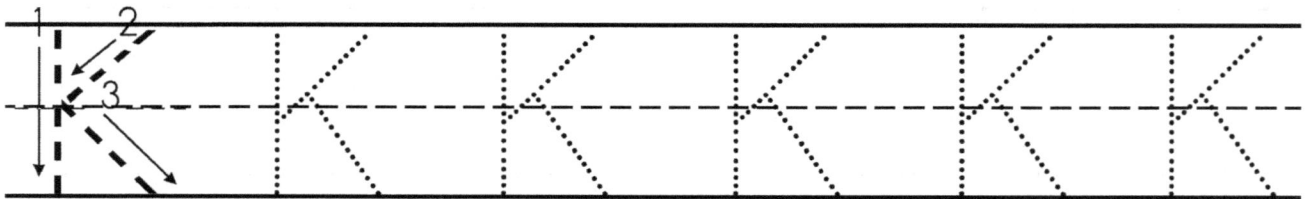

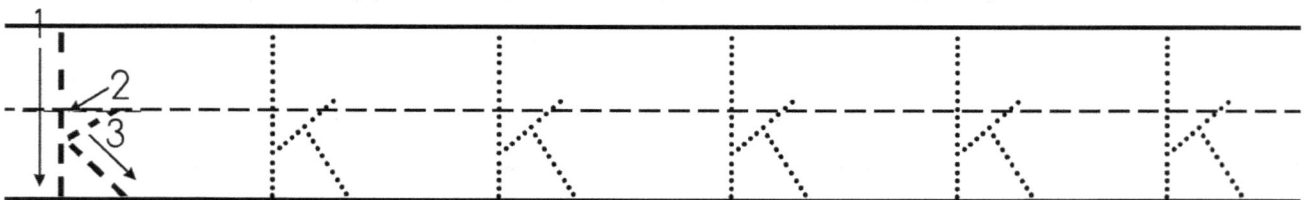

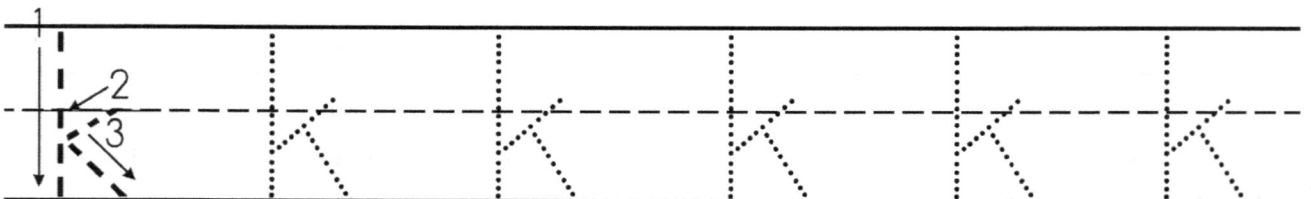

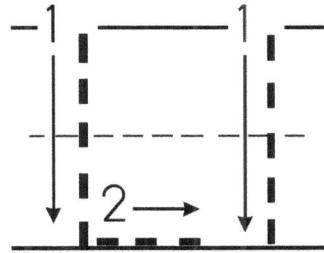

Lion

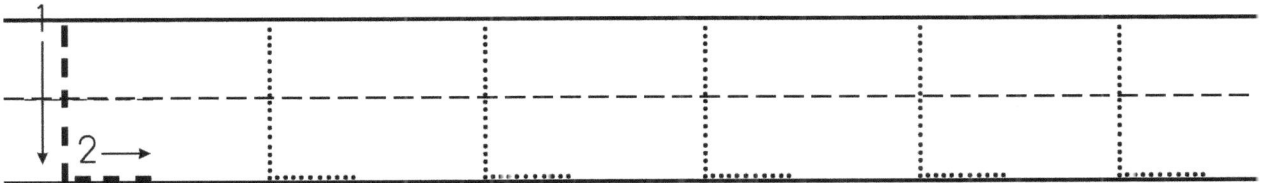

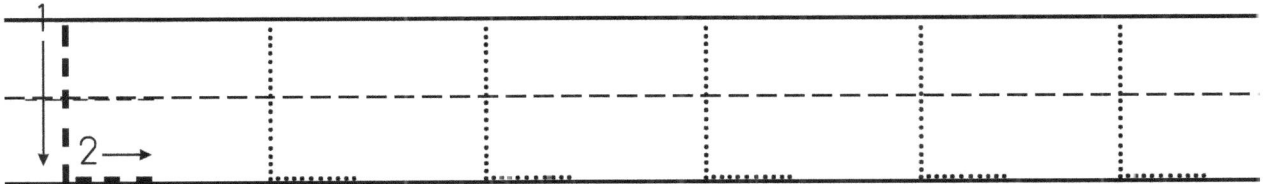

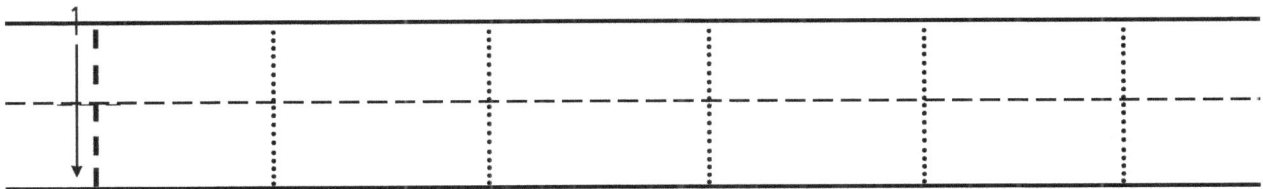

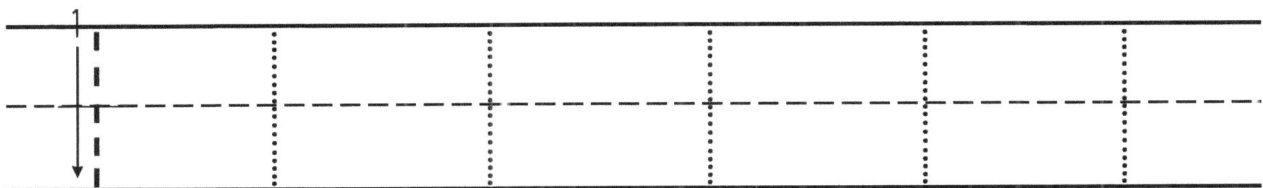

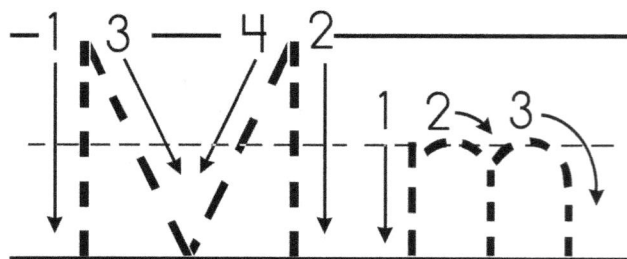

Mat

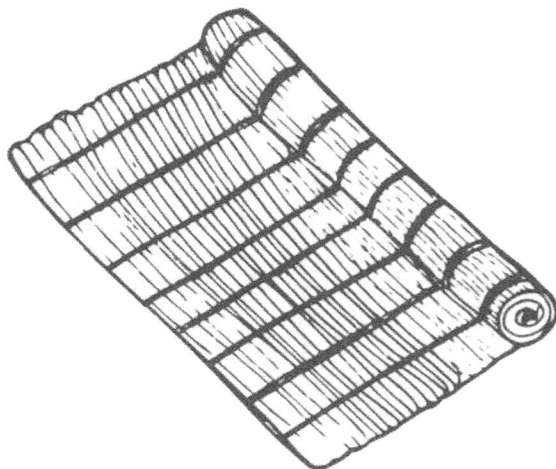

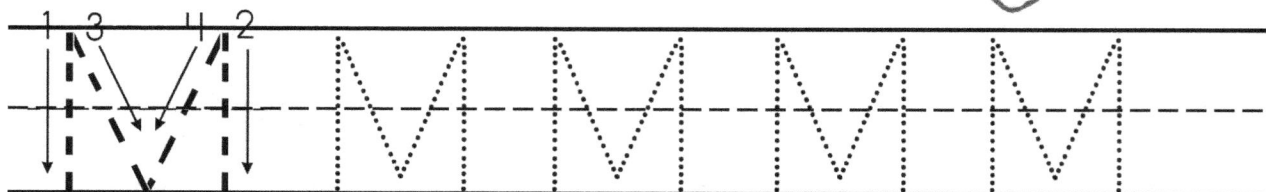

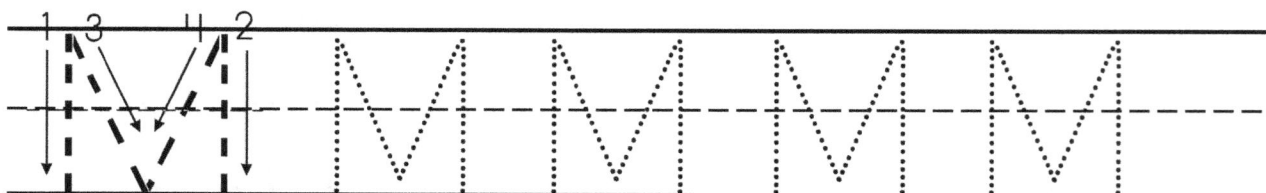

26

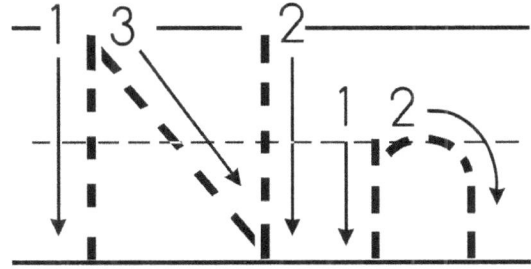

N**est**

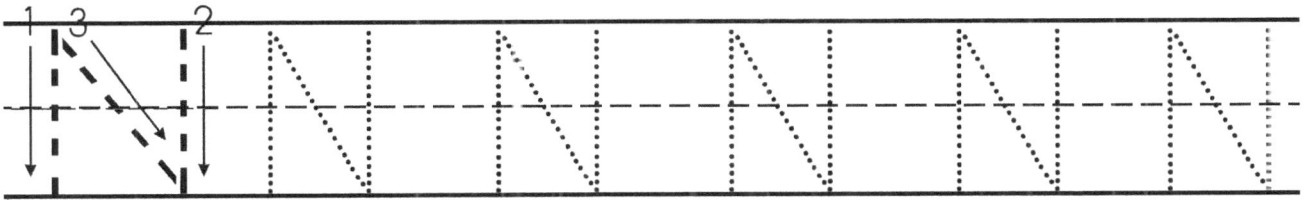

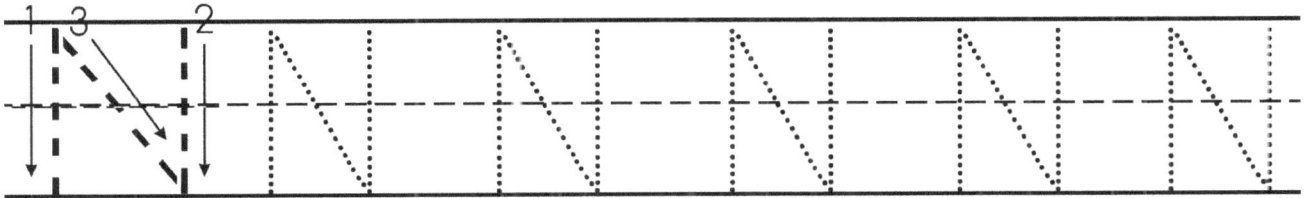

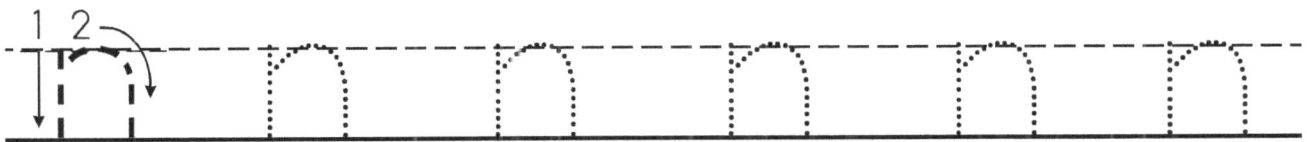

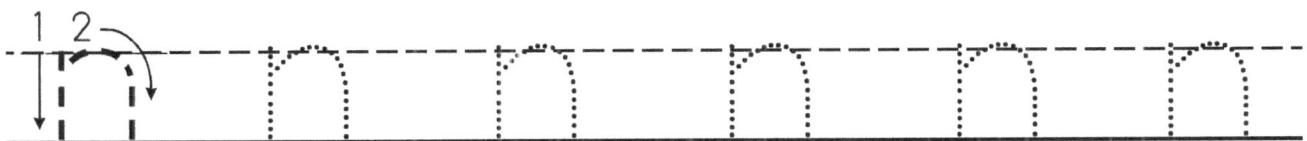

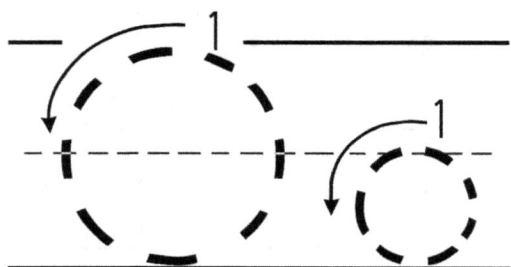

Owl

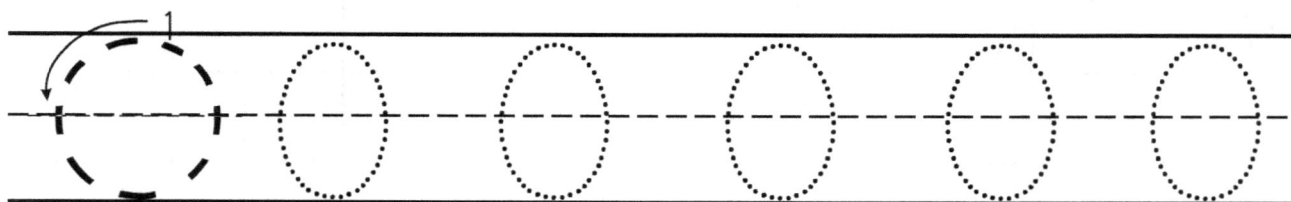

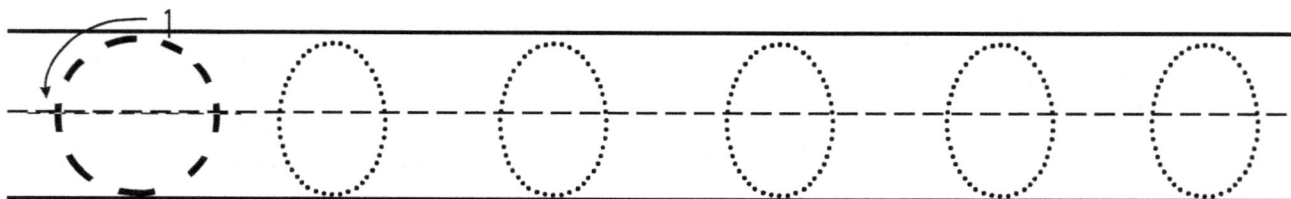

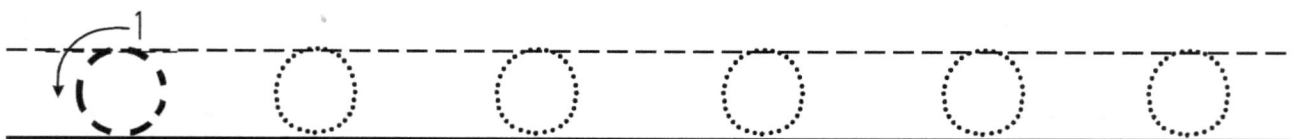

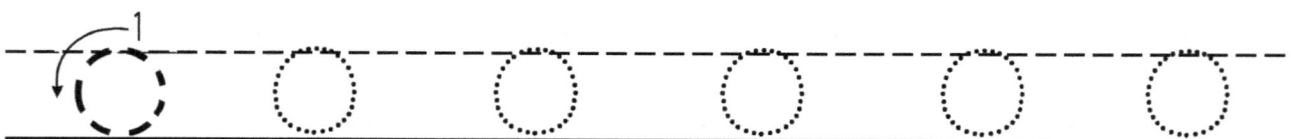

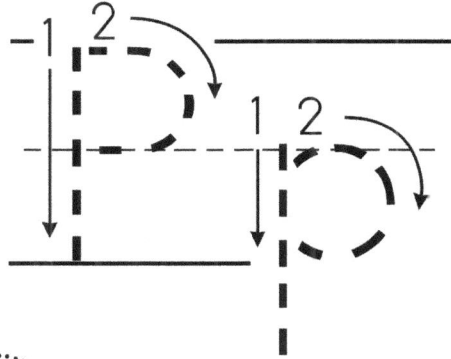

Pig

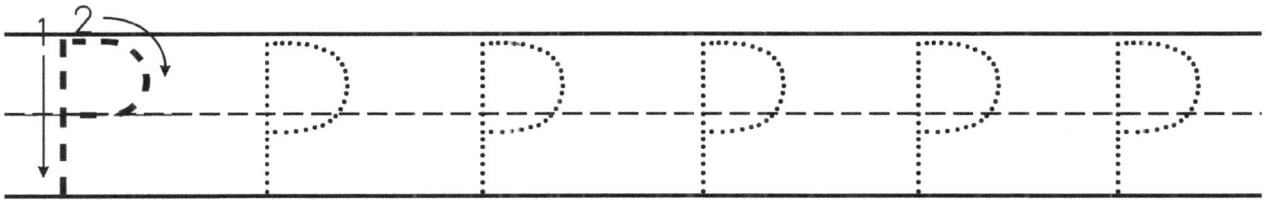

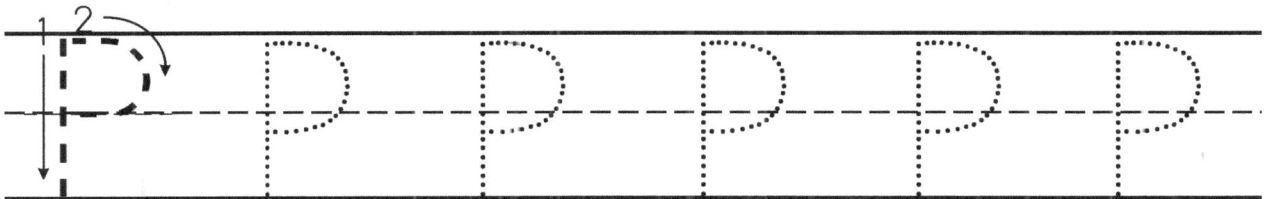

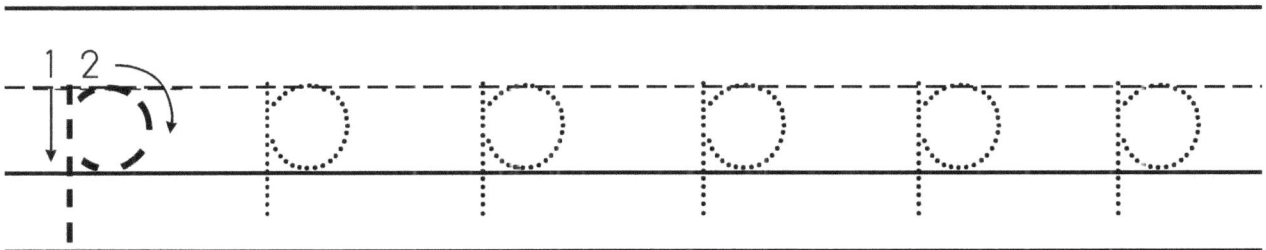

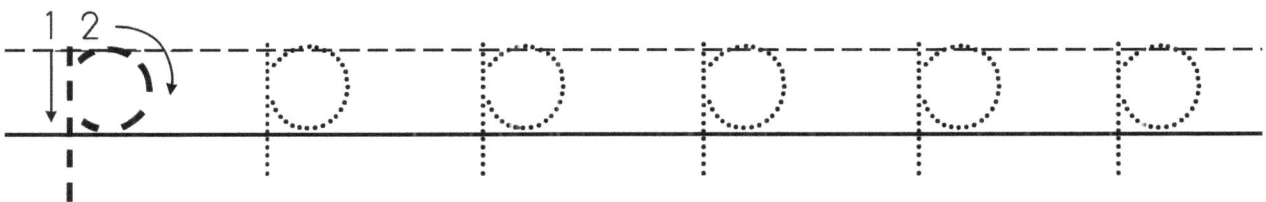

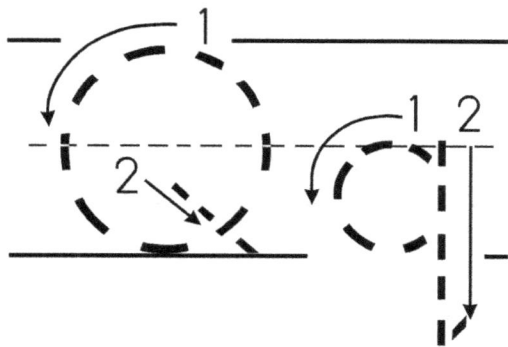

Queen

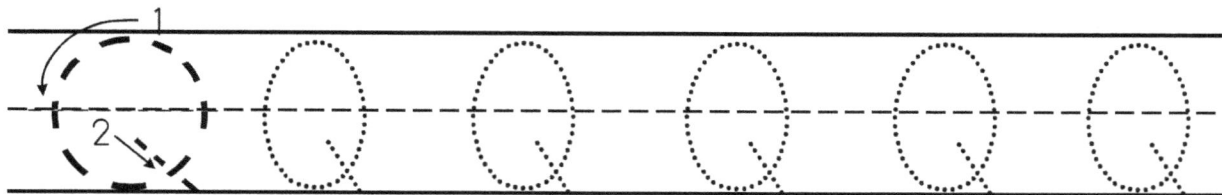

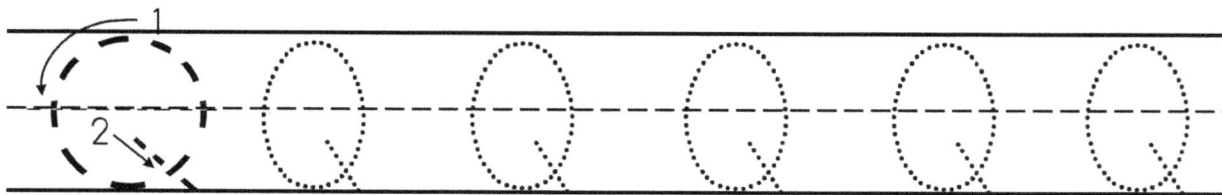

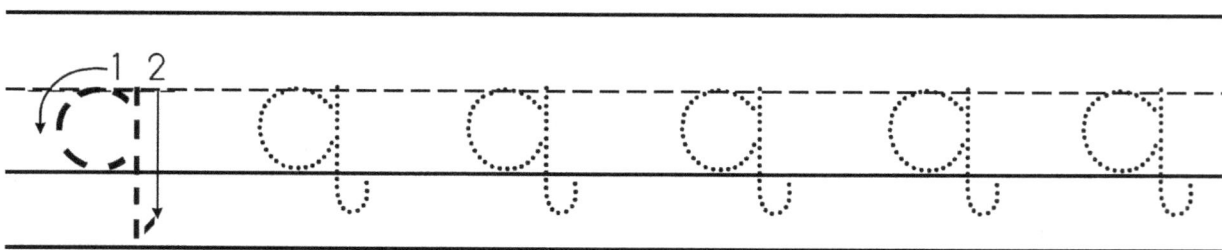

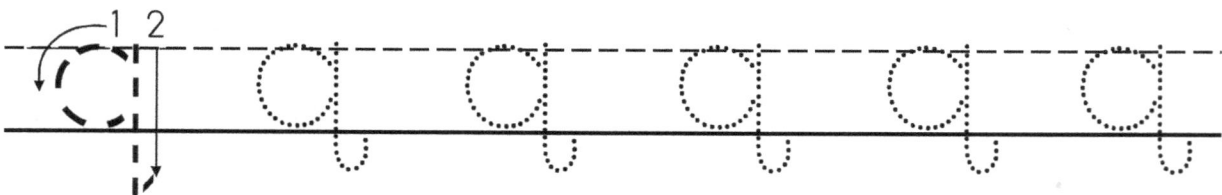

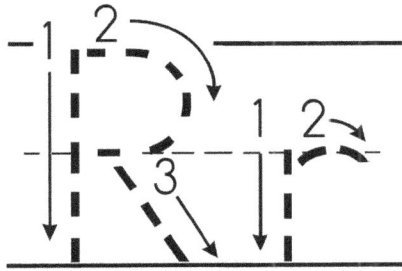

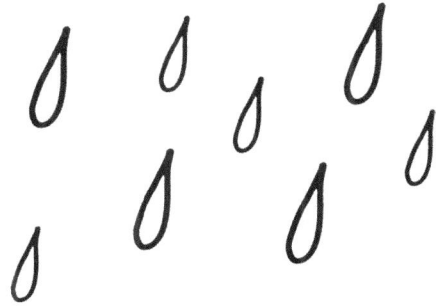

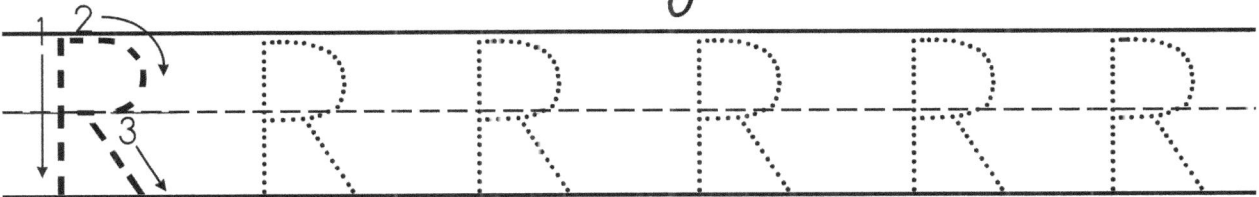

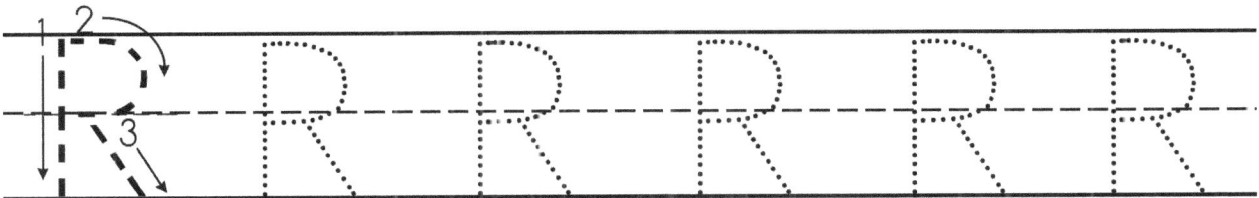

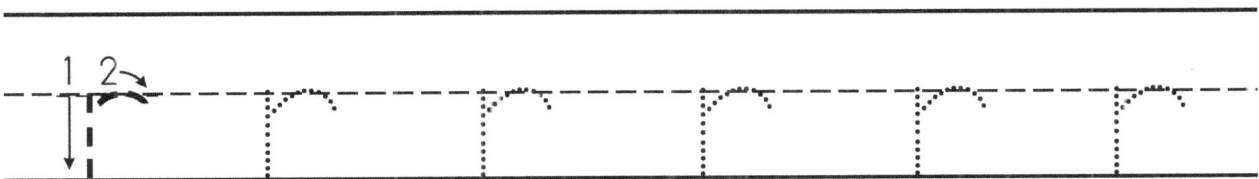

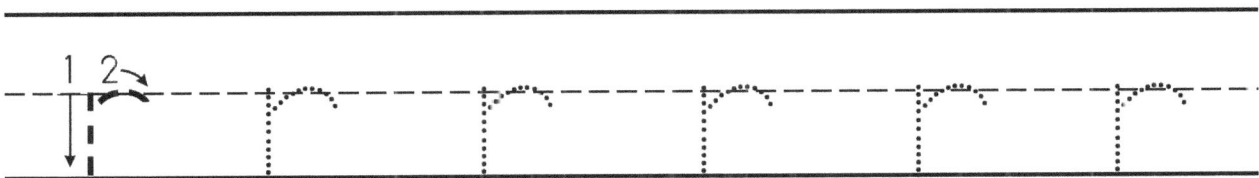

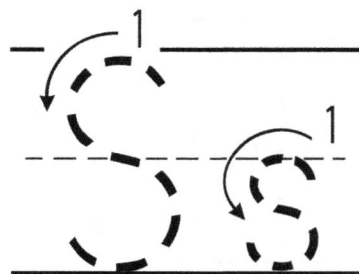

Sun

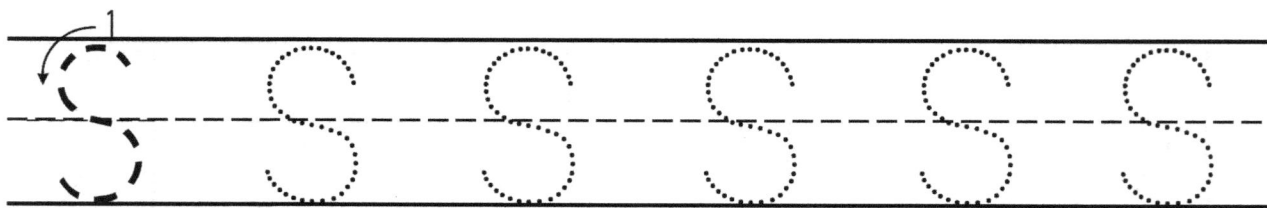

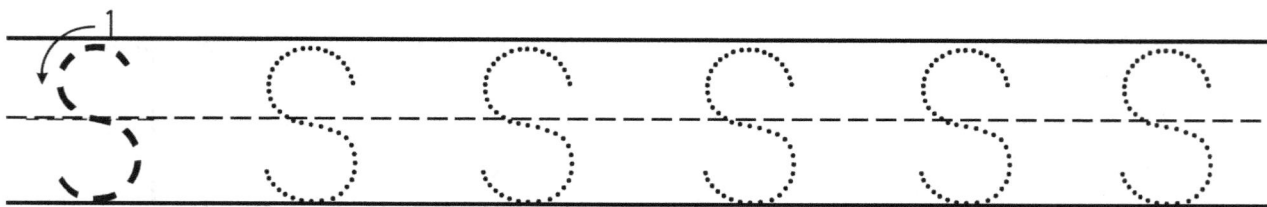

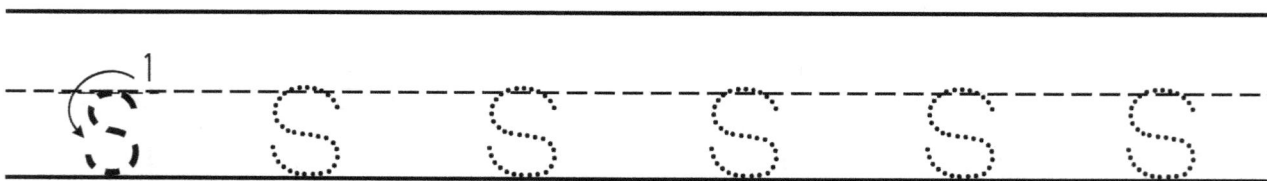

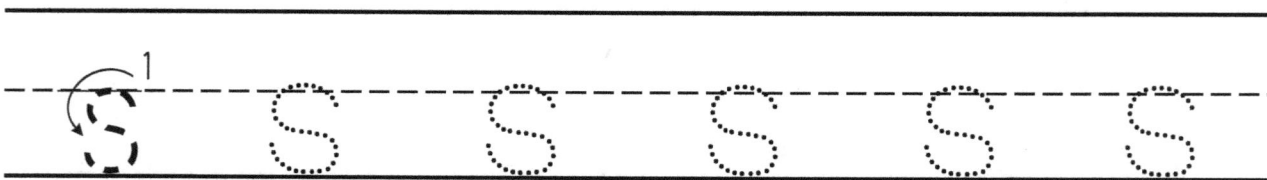

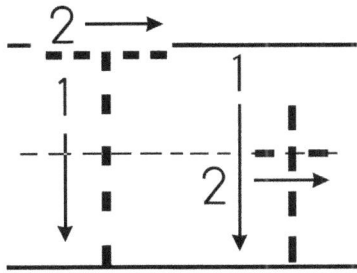

Tree

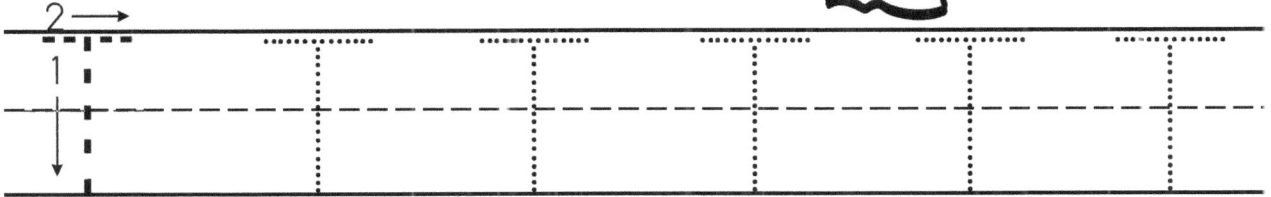

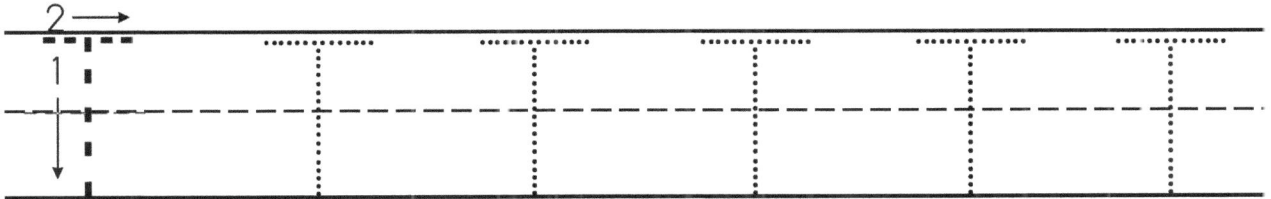

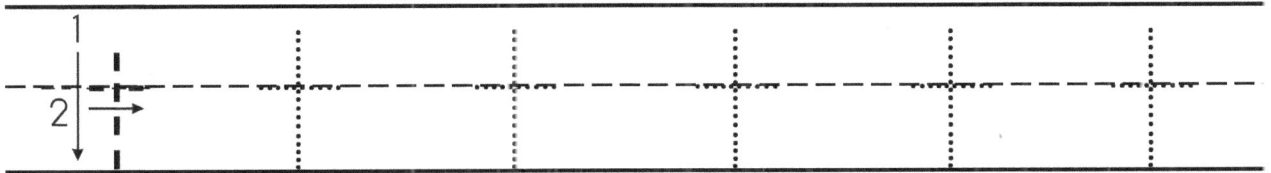

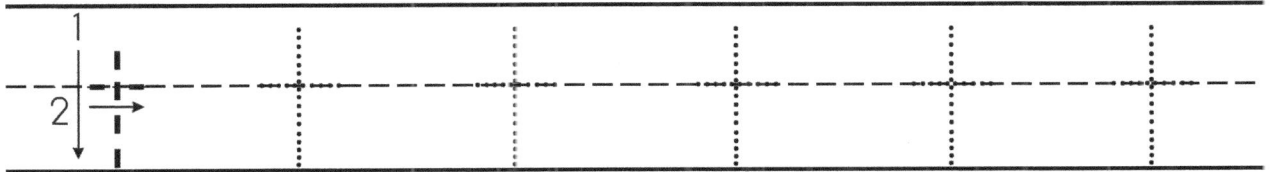

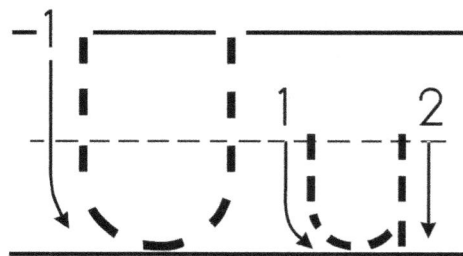

Umbrella

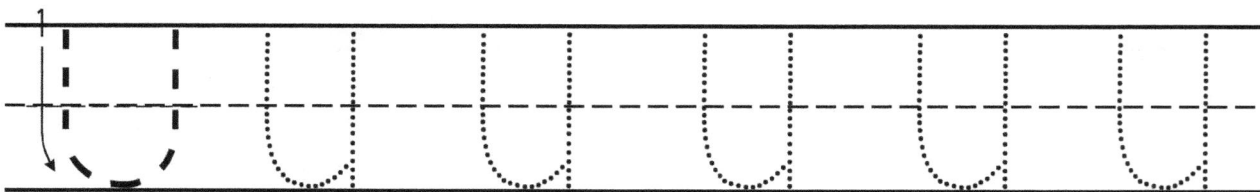

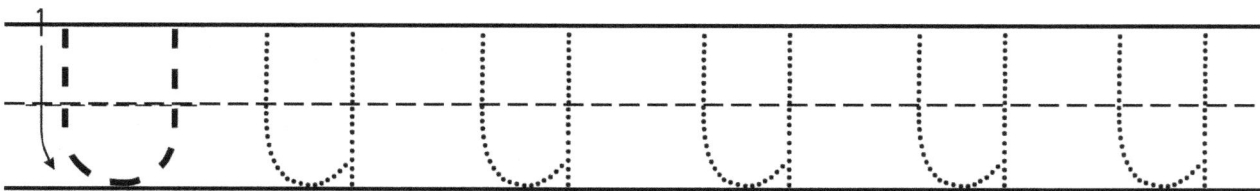

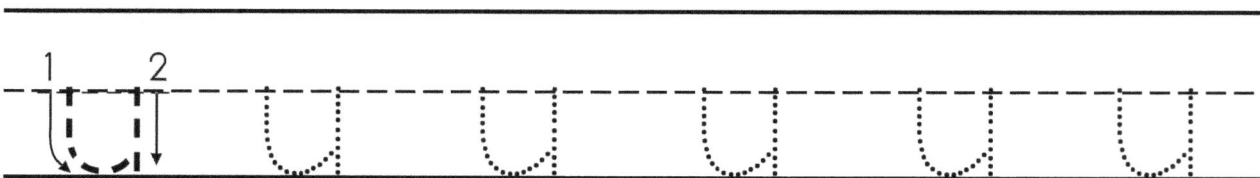

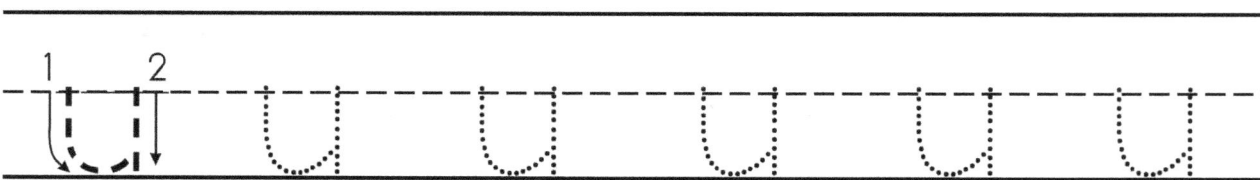

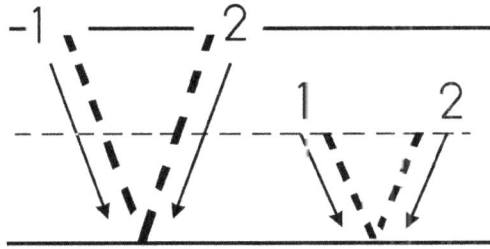

Van

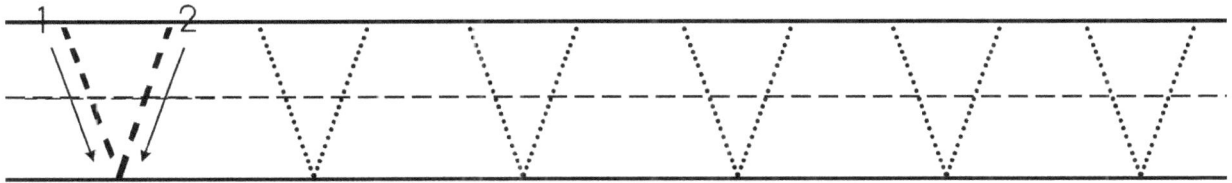

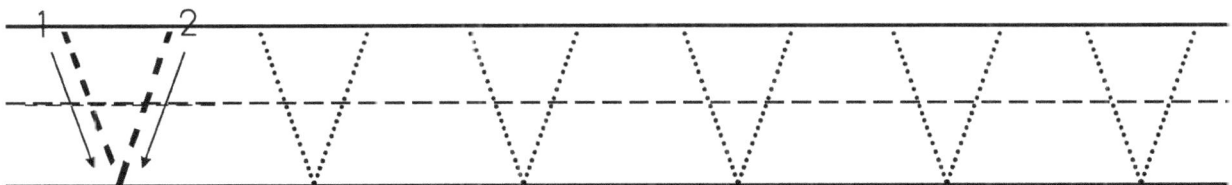

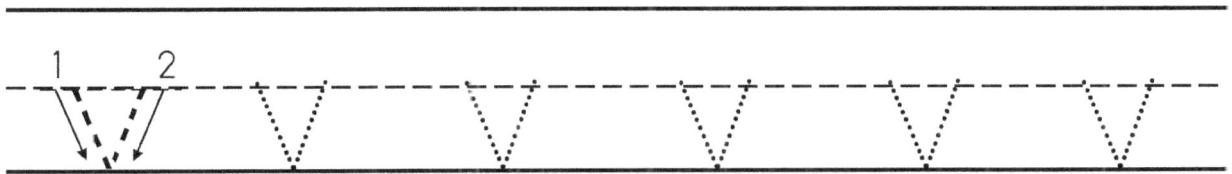

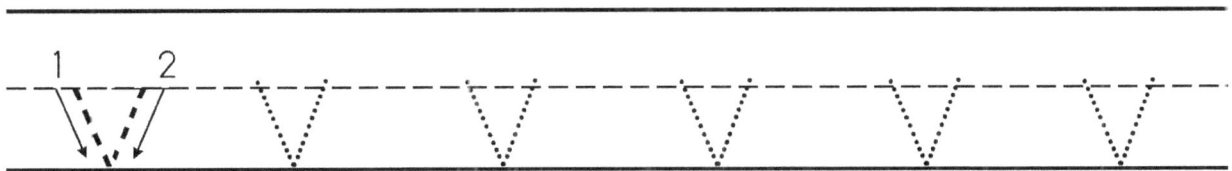

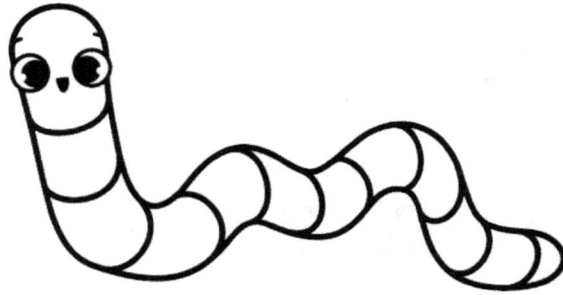

Worm

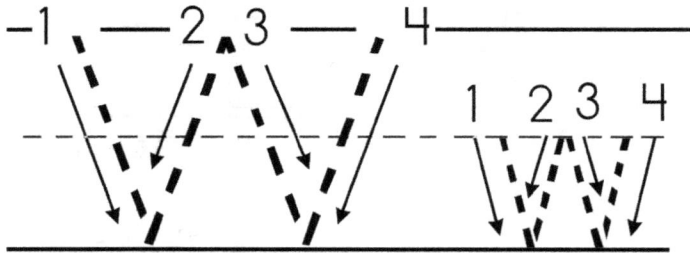

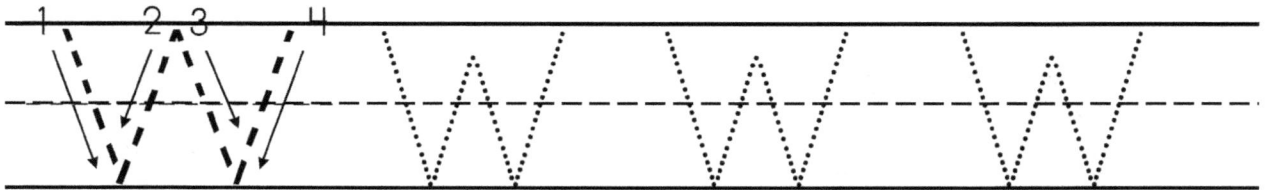

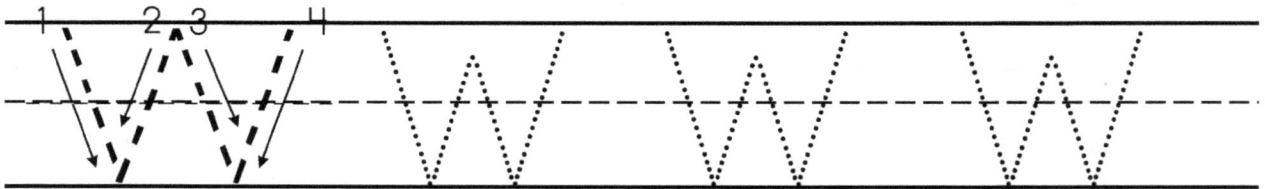

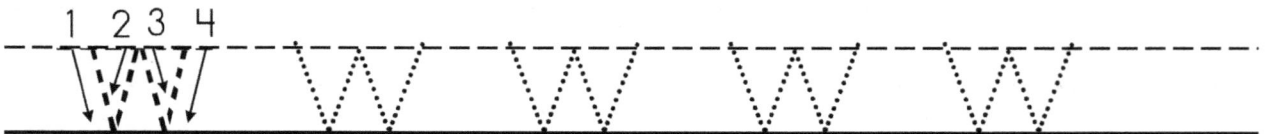

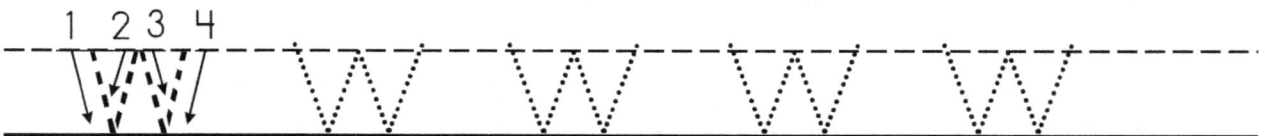

36

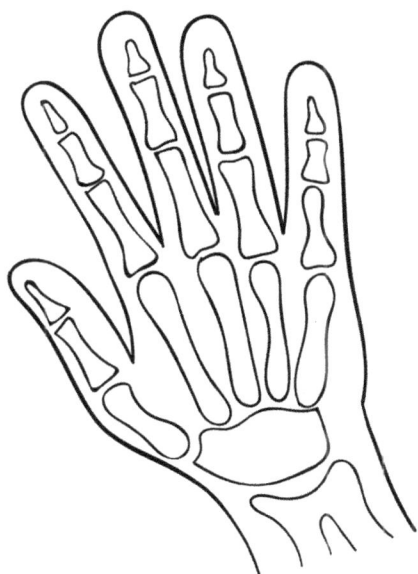

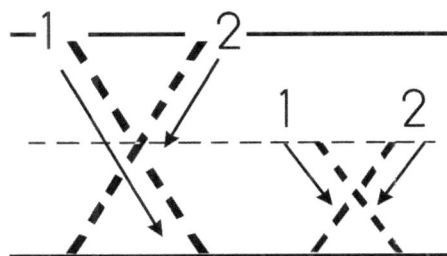

X**ray**

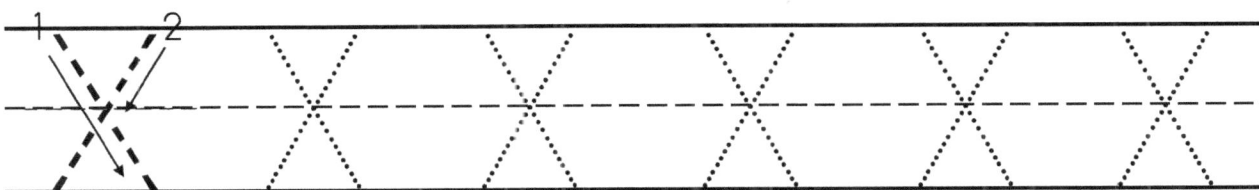

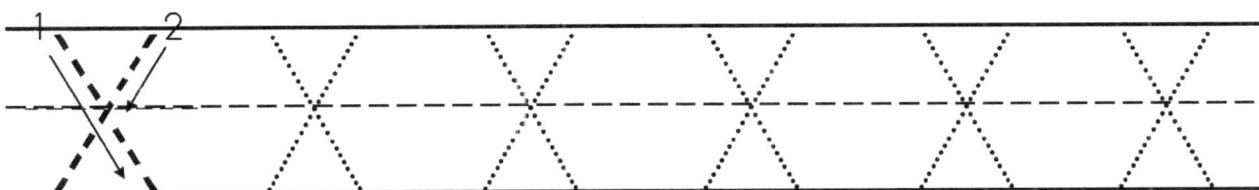

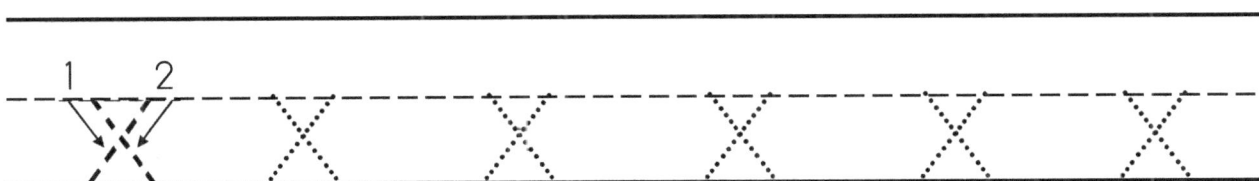

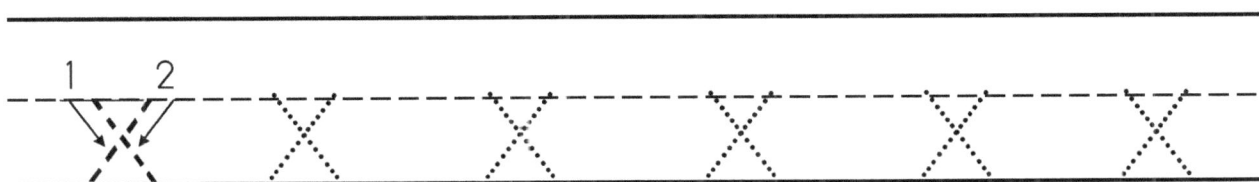

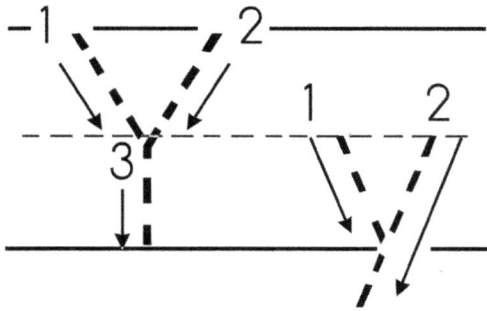
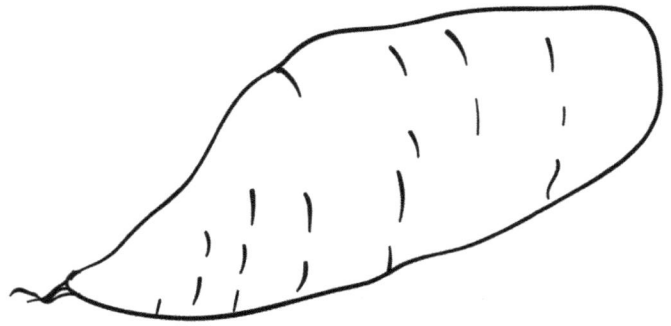

Yam

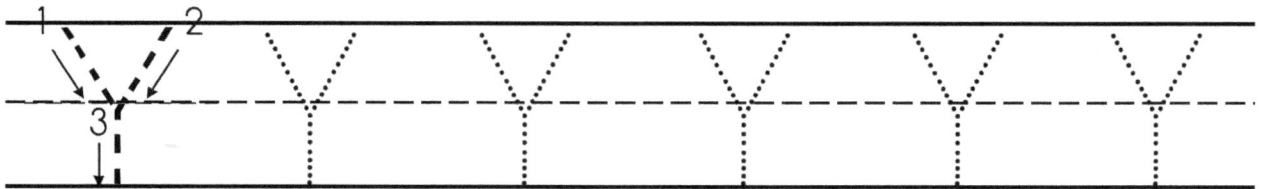
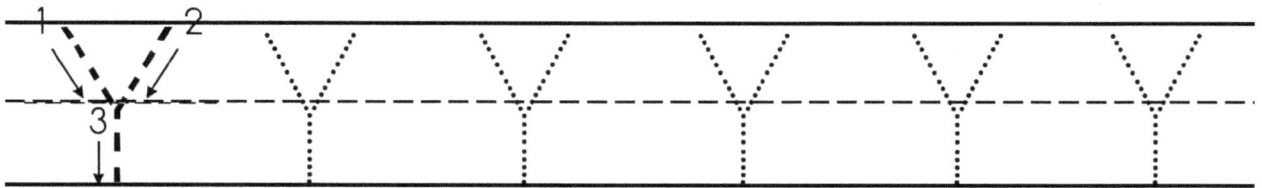
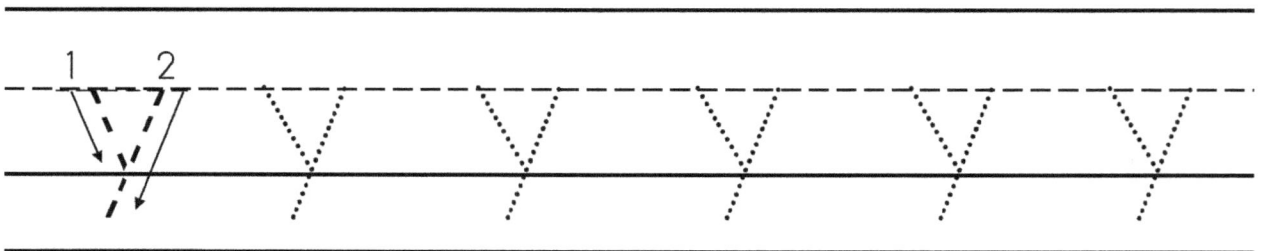
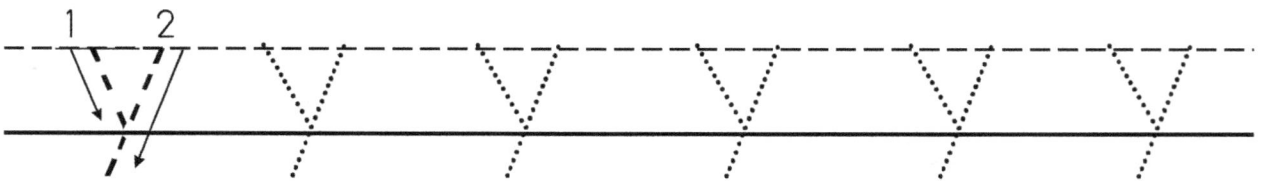

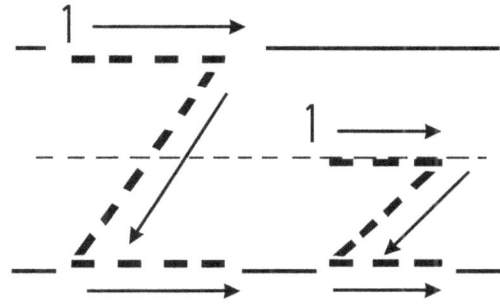

Zebra

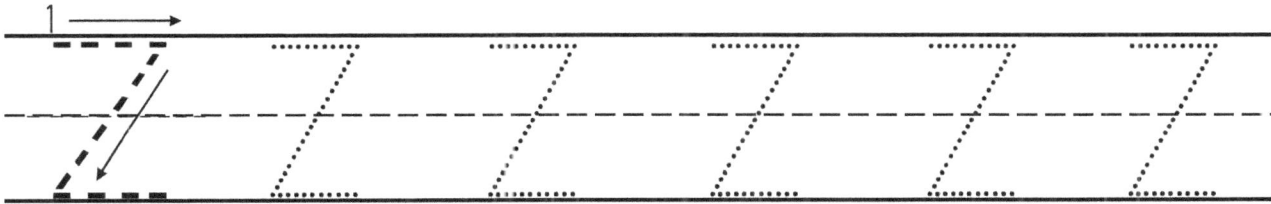

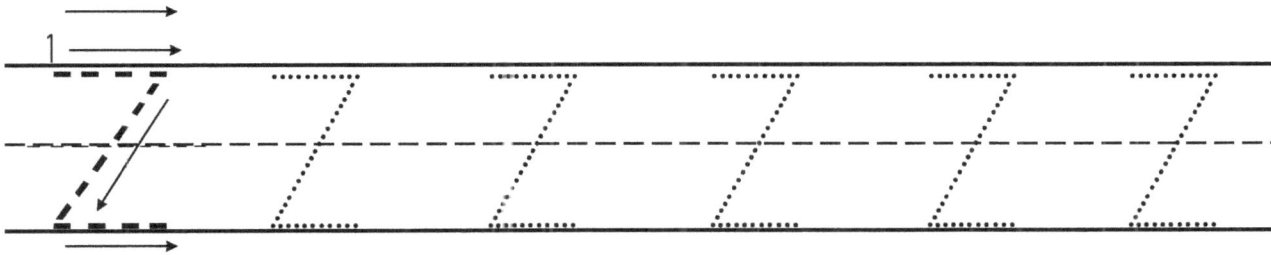

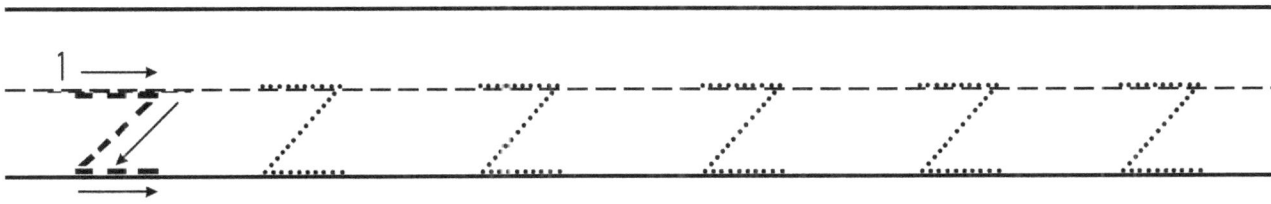

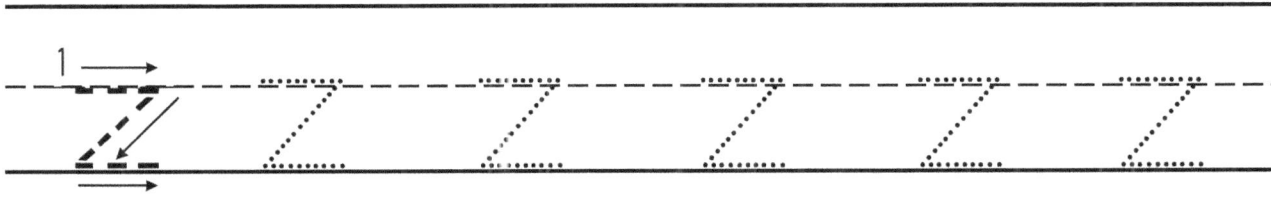

Trace the Uppercase Letters

A B C D E

F G H I J K

L M N O P

Q R S T U

V W X Y Z

Trace the Lowercase Letters

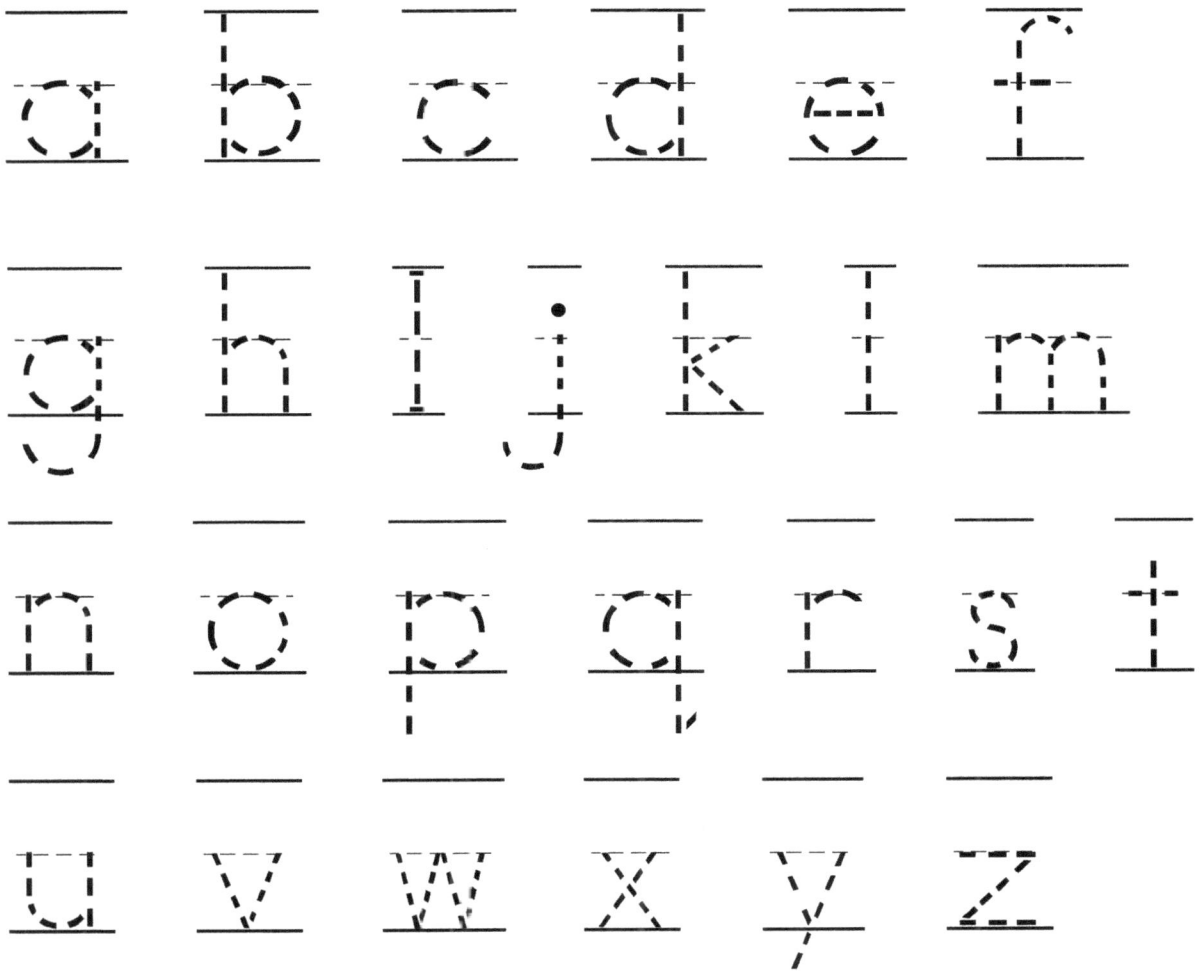

a b c d e f

g h i j k l m

n o p q r s t

u v w x y z

I Can Write My ABC's

A a B b C c D d E e

E e F f G g H h I i

J j K k L l M m N n

O o P p Q q R r S s

T t U u V v W w X x

Y y Z z

This time, let's try writing independently.

Try writing your ABC's independently.

I Can Write My ABC's

I Can Write My ABC's

I Can Write My ABC's

I can learn to spell my First Name

I can learn to spell my Last Name

Try writing your First Name independently.

Try writing your Last Name independently.

Write your name in UPPERCASE letters:

Write your name in lowercase letters:

Name: _____

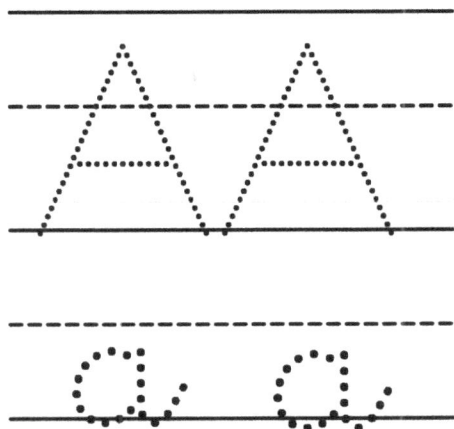

Find the Letters

Trace the letters. Then color the circles that have the letter you traced.

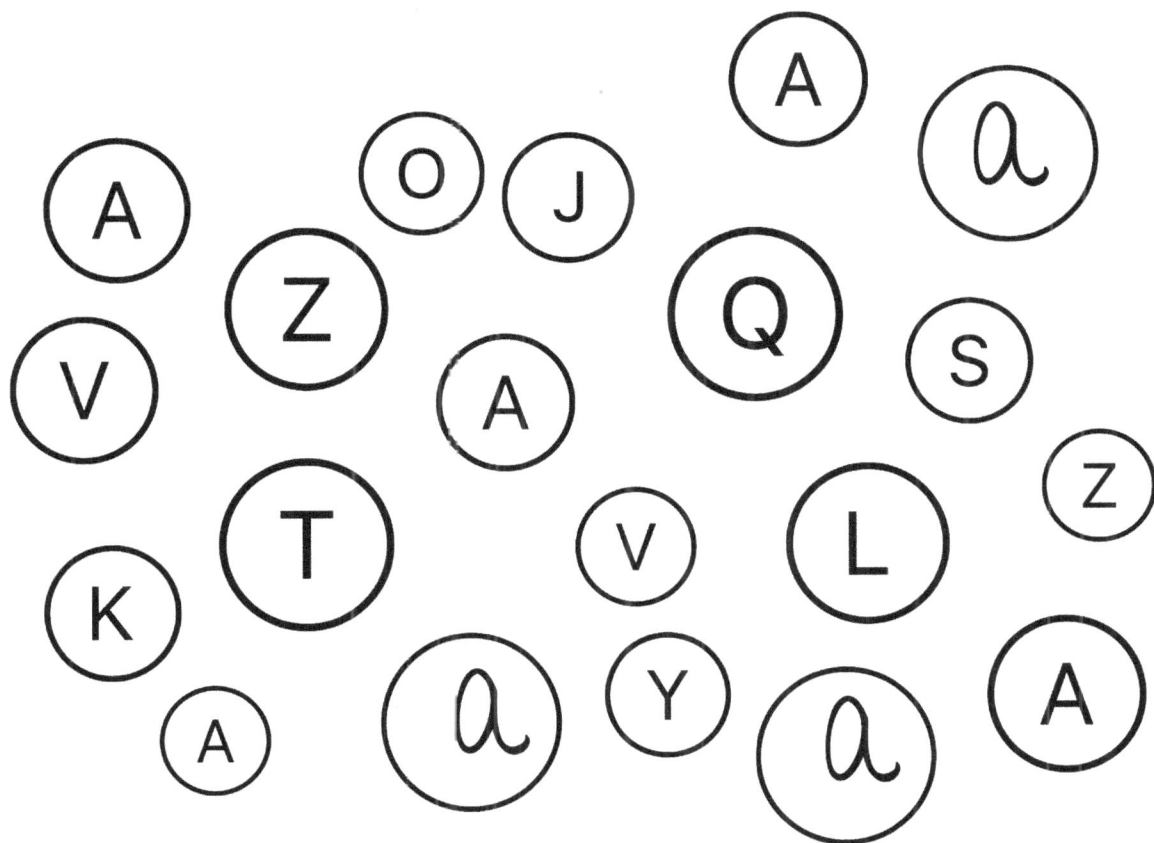

A A

a a

Name: ....

B B

b b

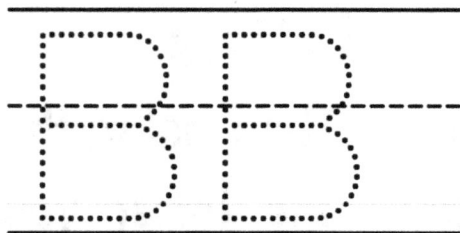

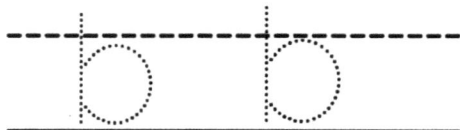

Find the letters

Trace the letters. Then color the circles that have the letter you traced.

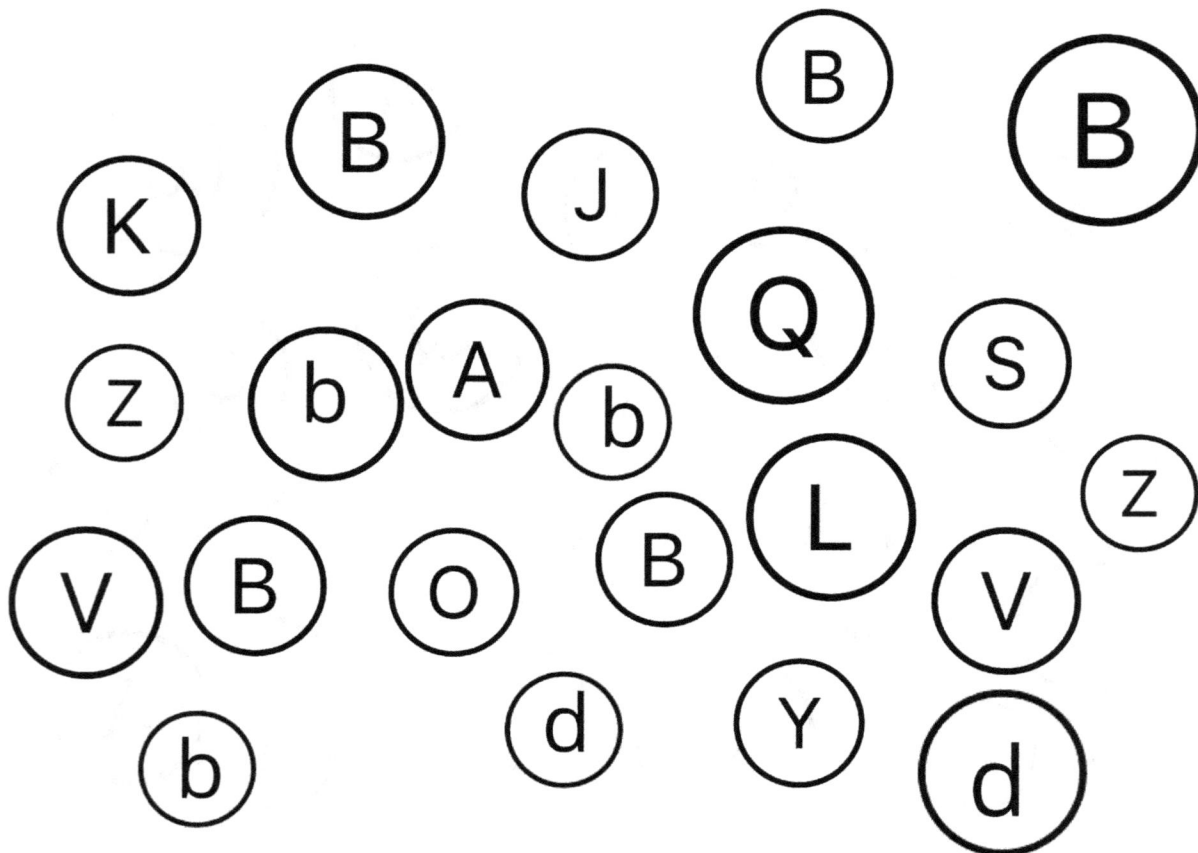

K   B   J   B   B

Z   b   A   b   Q   S

V   B   O   B   L   Z   V

b   d   Y   d

Name: _____

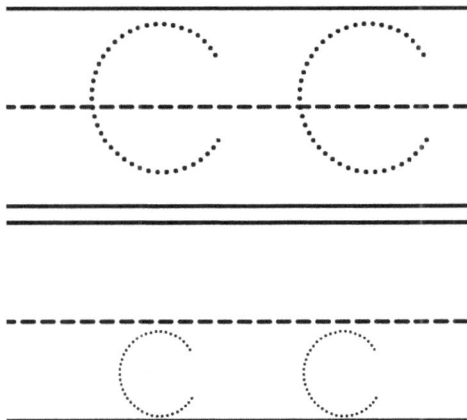

Find the Letters

Trace the letters. Then color the circles that have the letter you traced.

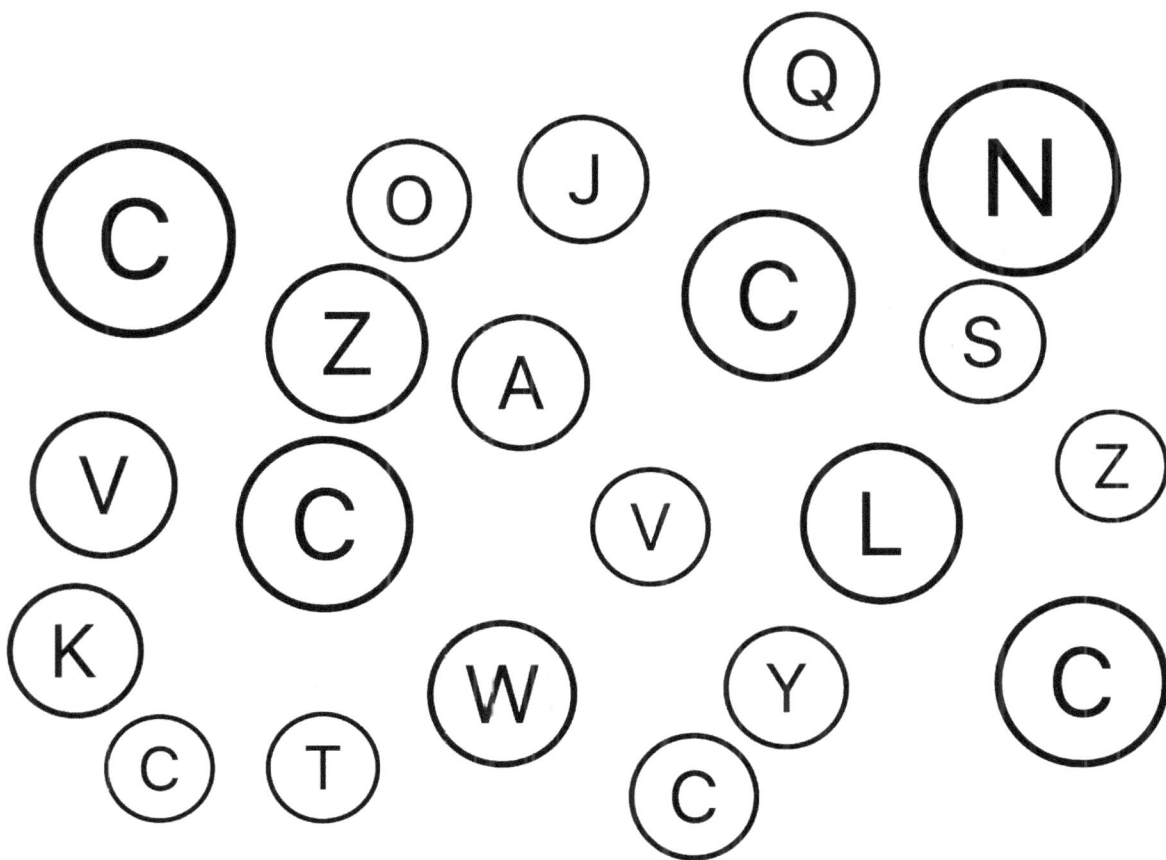

C C

c c

Name:

D D

d d

Find the letters

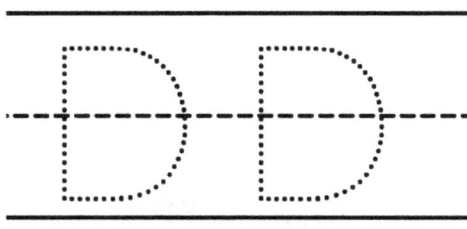

Trace the letters. Then color the circles that have the letter you traced.

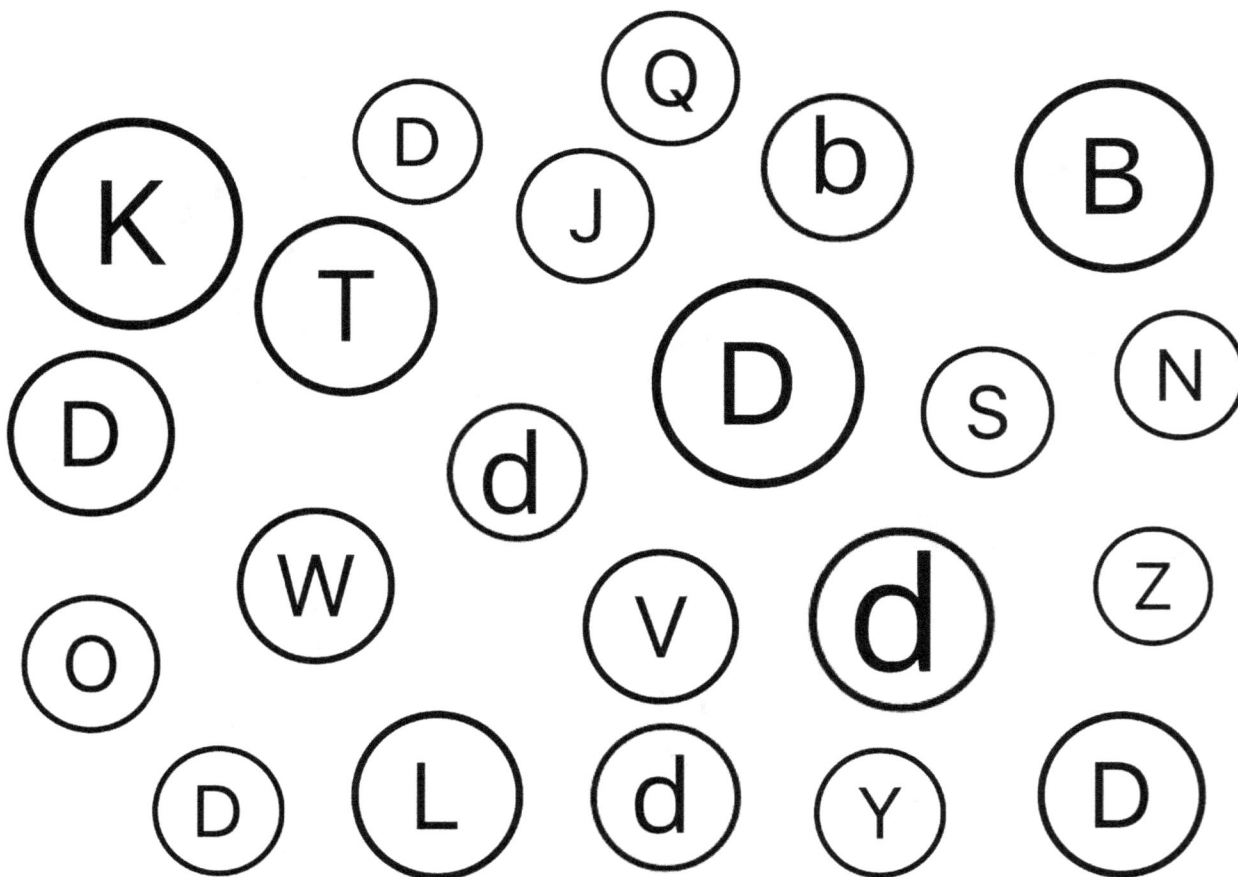

K D Q J b B
T D D S N
D d D
W V d Z
O
D L d Y D

Name:

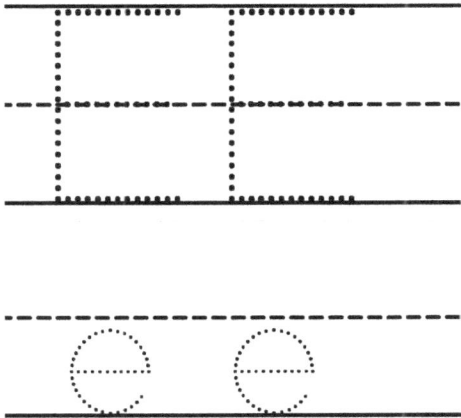

Find the Letters

Trace the letters. Then color the circles that have the letter you traced.

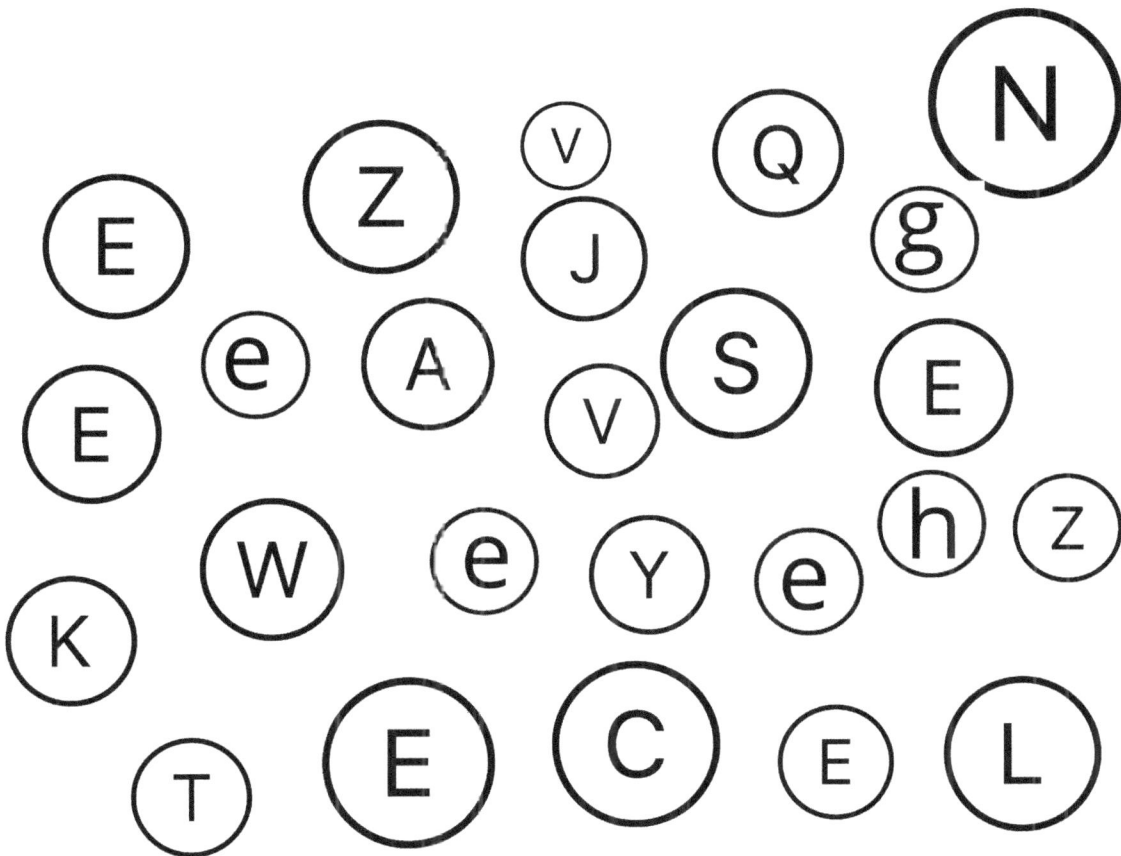

Name:

F F

f f

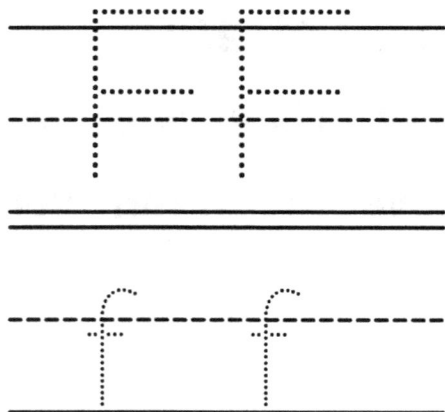

Find the letters

Trace the letters. Then color the circles that have the letter you traced.

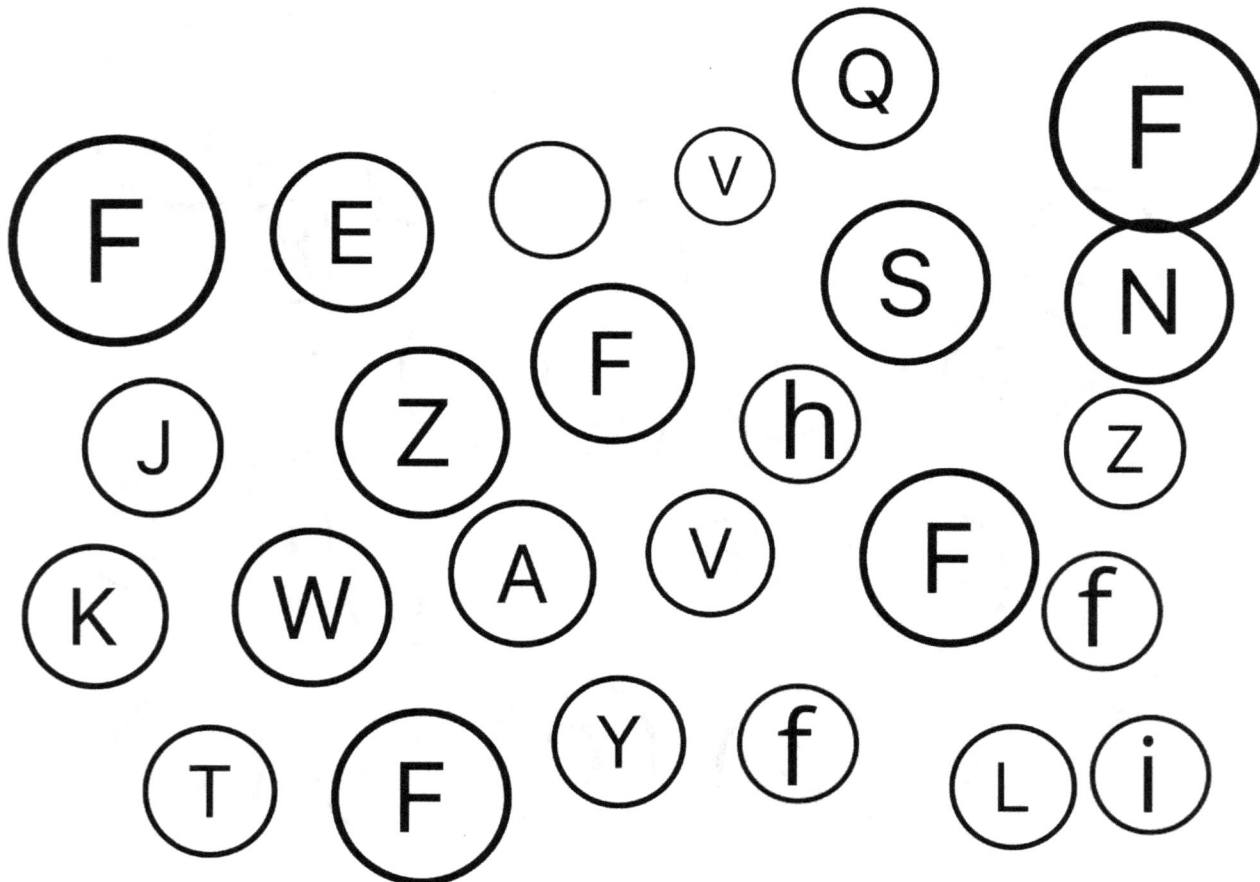

Name:

G G

g g

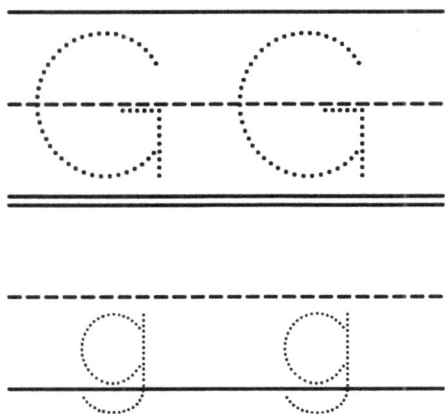

Find the Letters

Trace the letters. Then color the circles that have the letter you traced.

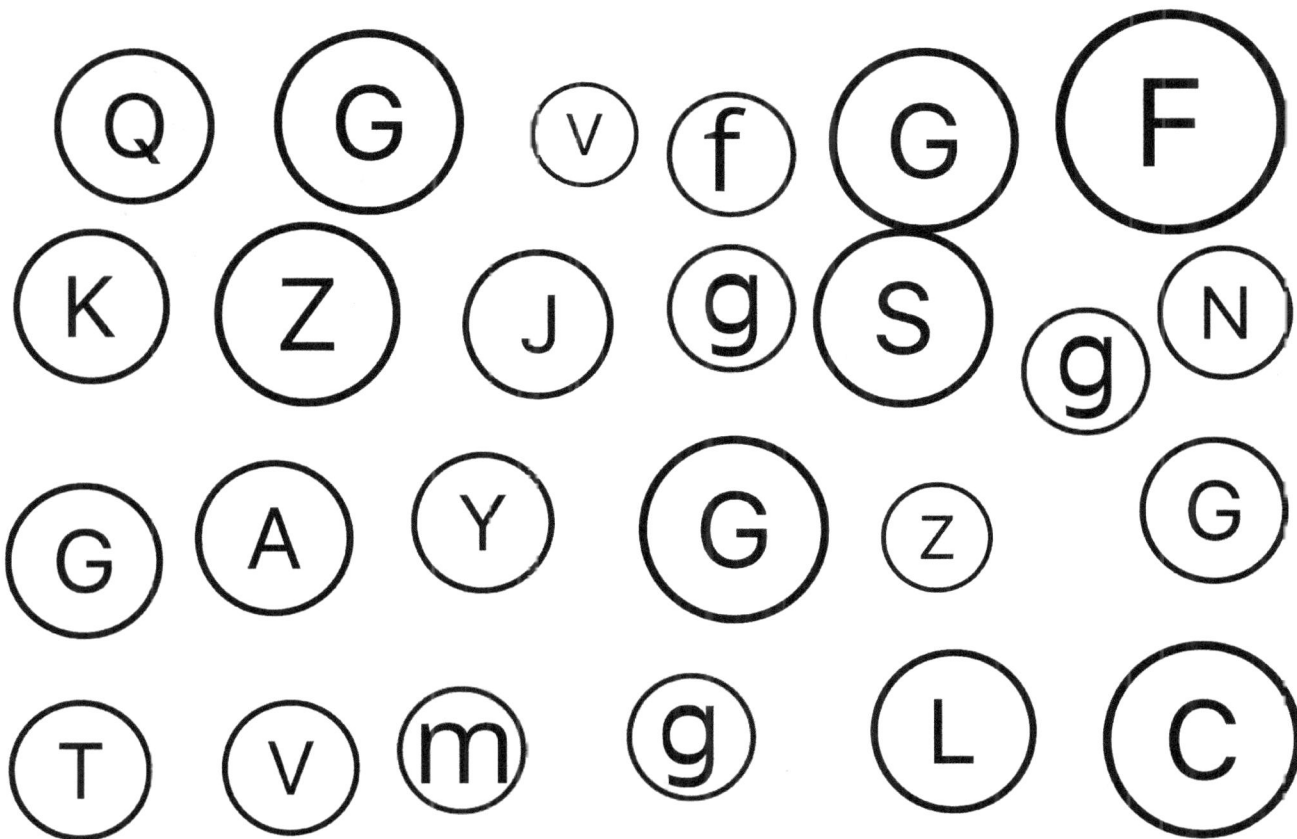

Q G v f G F

K Z J g S g N

G A Y G z G

T v m g L C

Name:

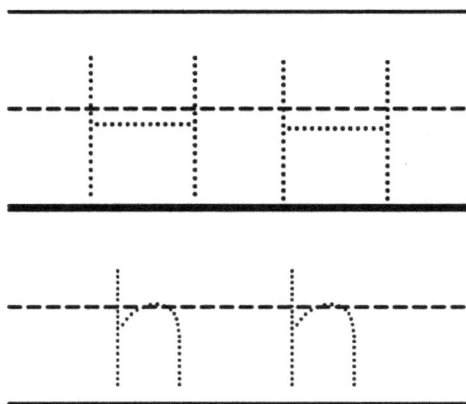

Find the letters

Trace the letters. Then color the circles that have the letter you traced.

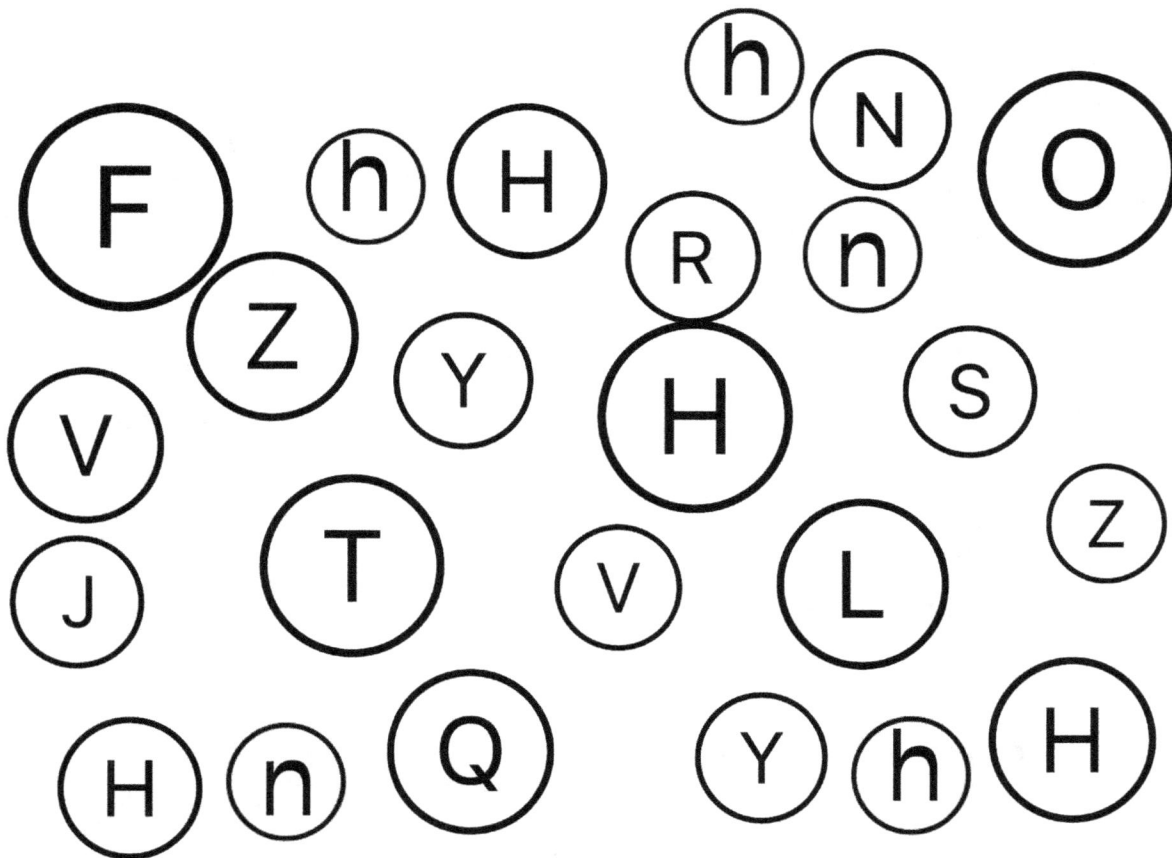

H H

h h

F h H h N O

Z R n

V Y H S

J T V L Z

H n Q Y h H

Name:

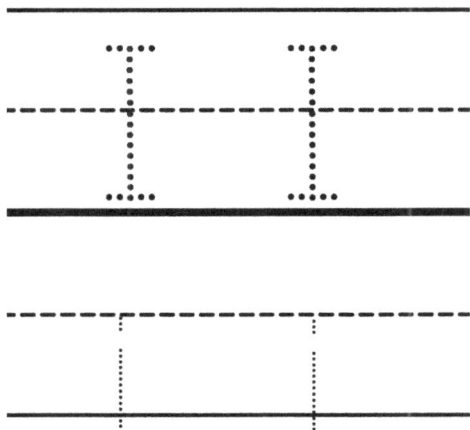

Find the Letters

Trace the letters. Then color the circles that have the letter you traced.

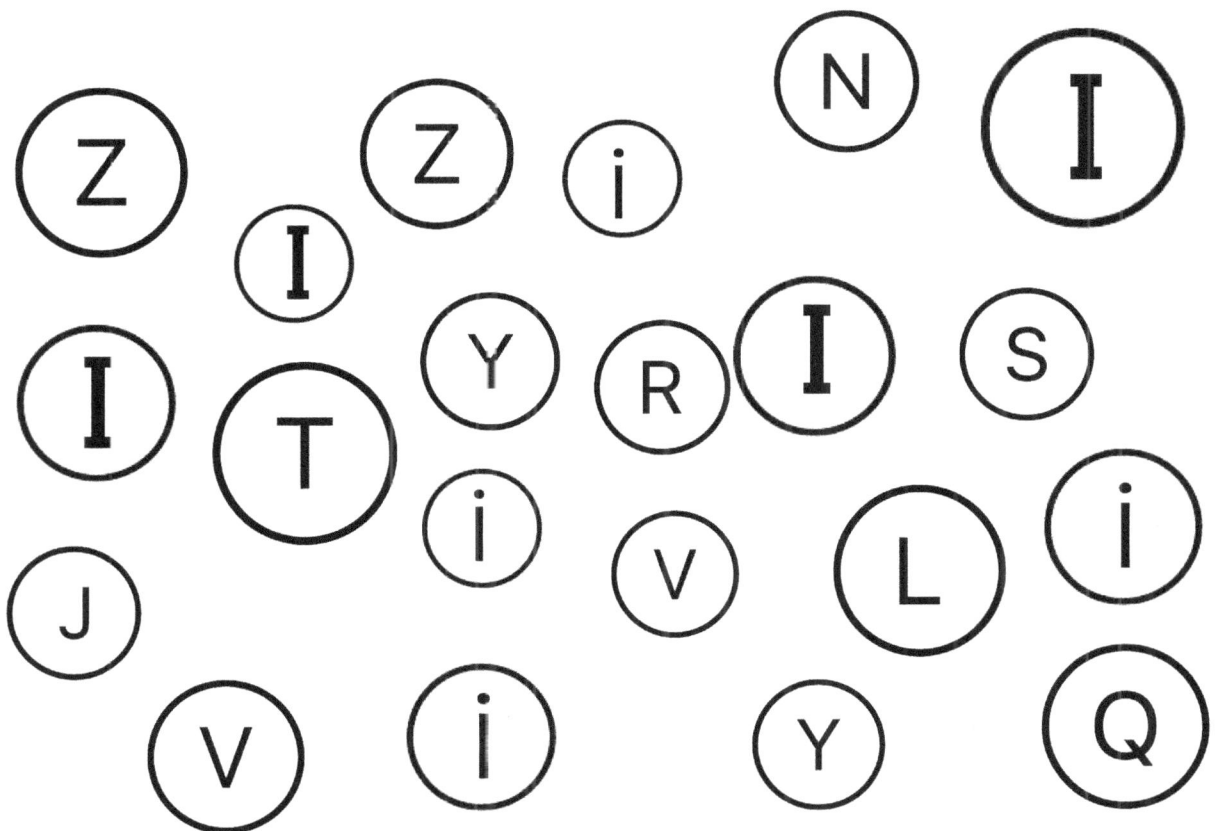

Z Z i N I

I

I Y R I S

T

i

V L i

J

V i Y Q

Name: _____

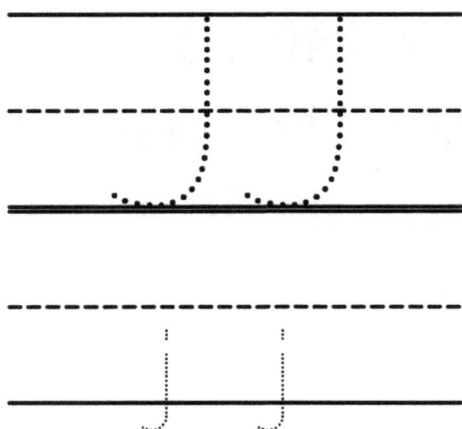

Find the letters

Trace the letters. Then color the circles that have the letter you traced.

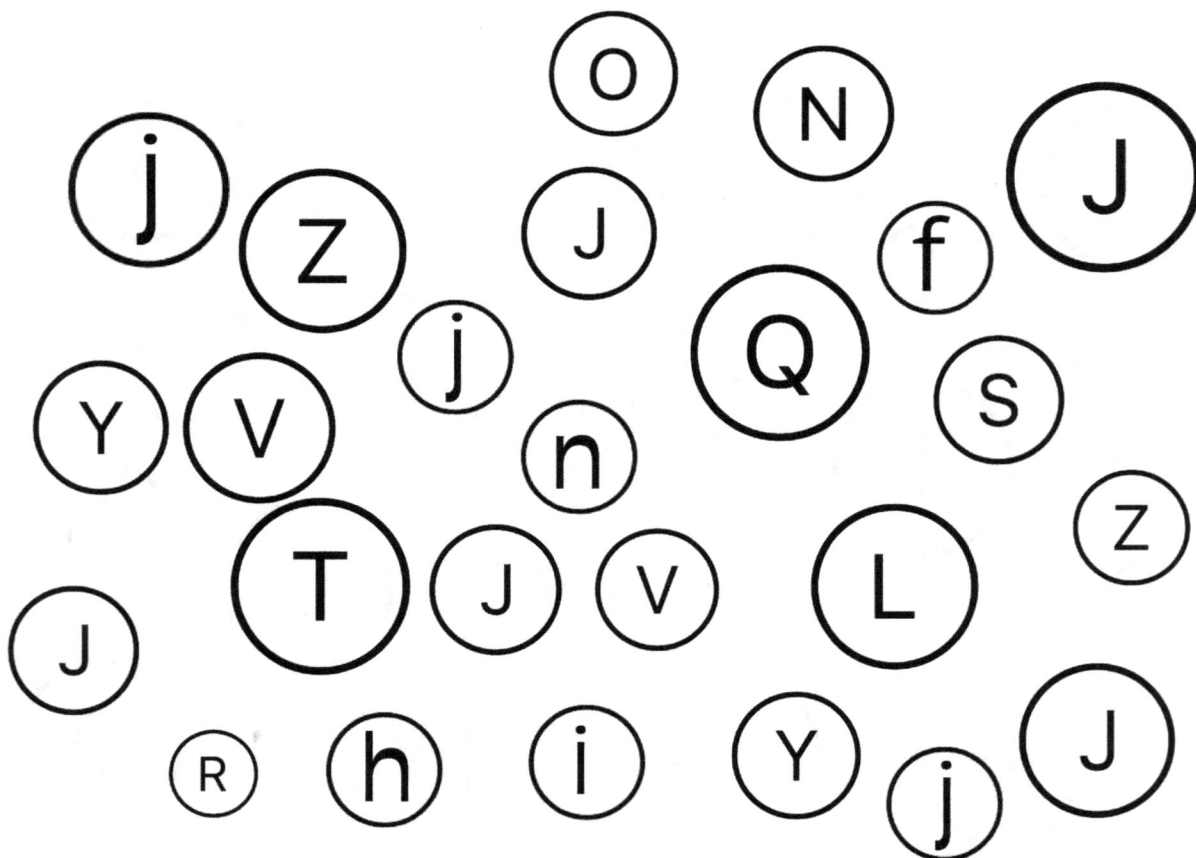

j z O N J
Y V j J f
J T n Q S
R h J V L Z
i Y j J

Name:

K K

k k

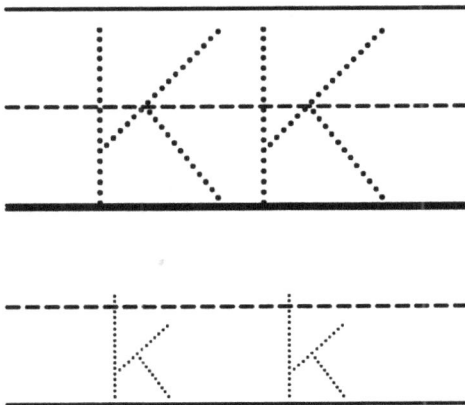

Find the Letters

Trace the letters. Then color the circles that have the letter you traced.

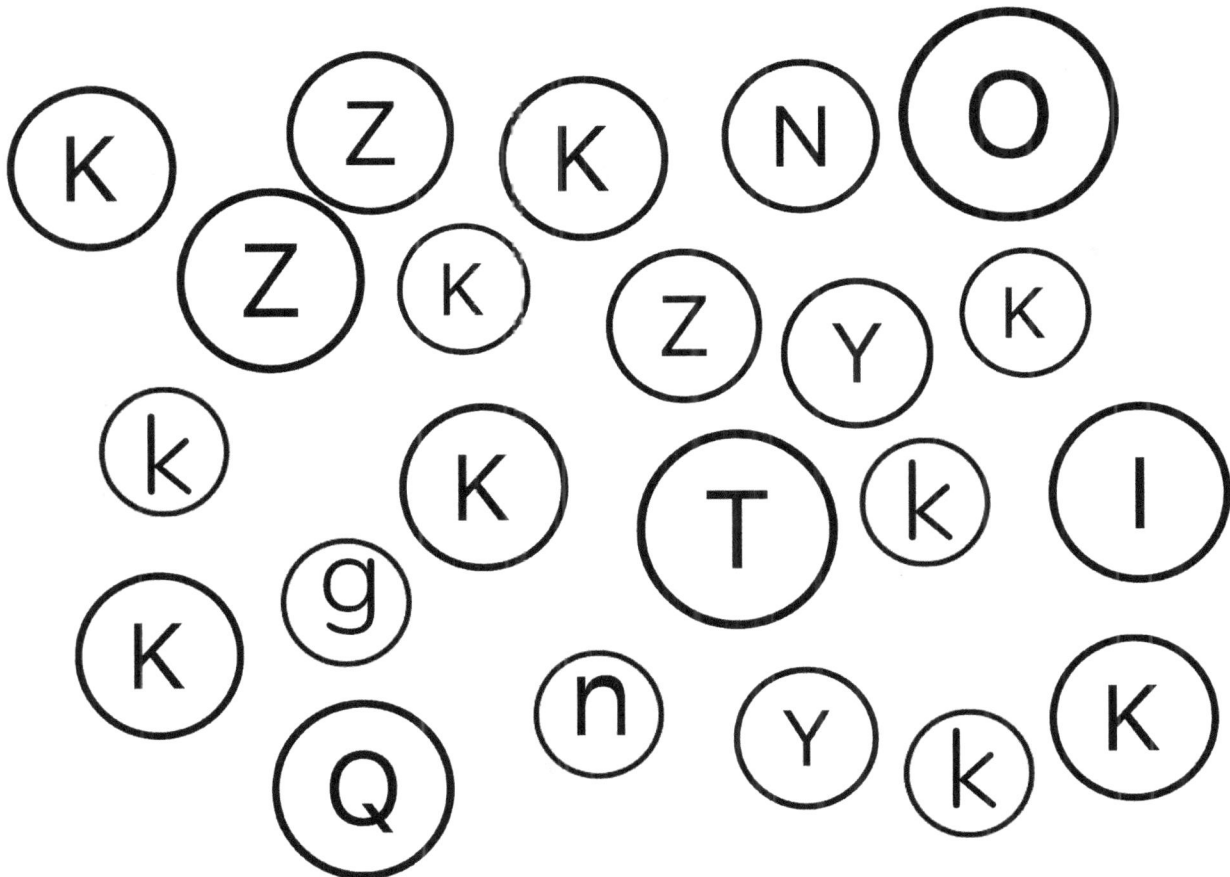

K Z K N O
Z k Z Y K
k K T k l
K g n Y k K
Q

Name:

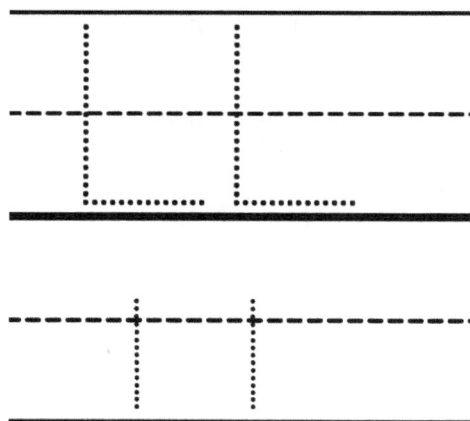

Find the letters

Trace the letters. Then color the circles that have the letter you traced.

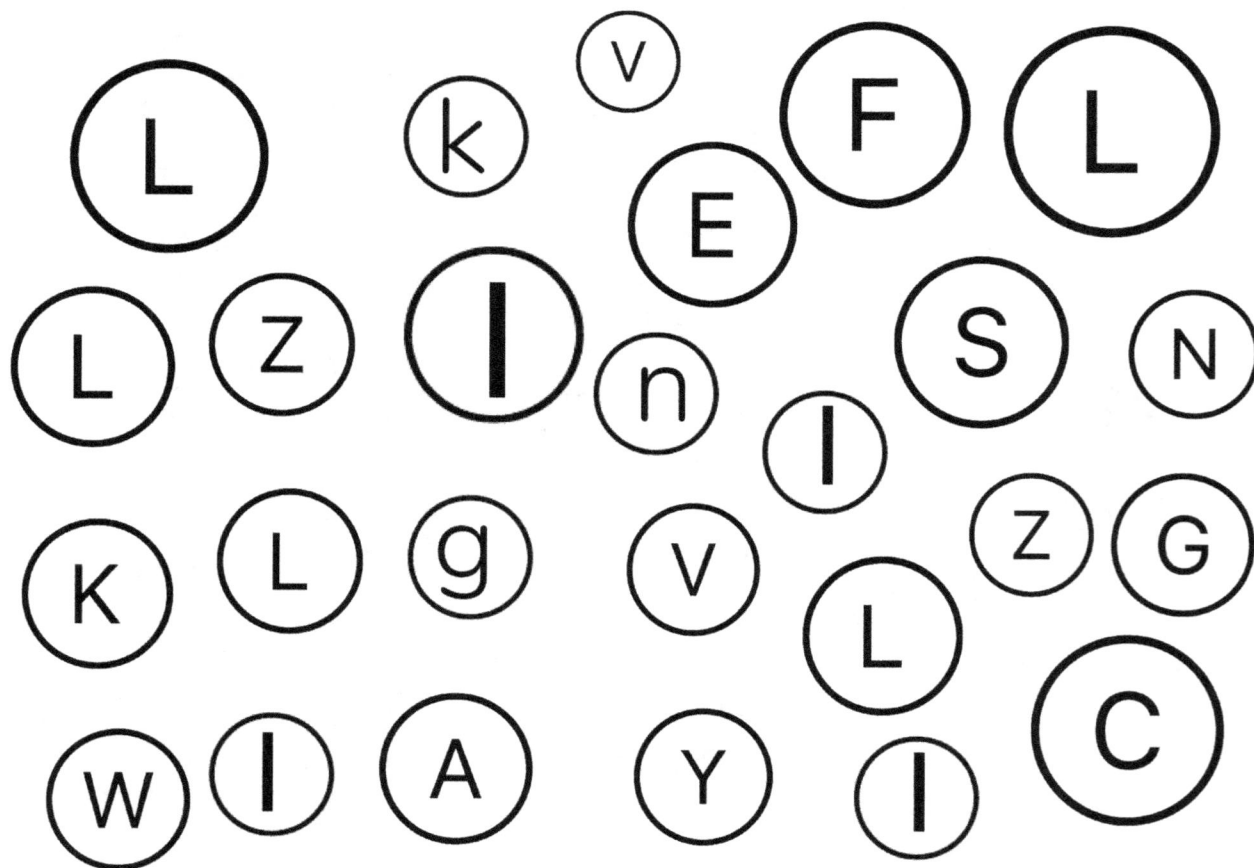

L   k   v   F   L

L   z   I   E   S   N

        n   I

K   L   g   v   Z   G

                L

W   I   A   Y   I   C

Name: _____

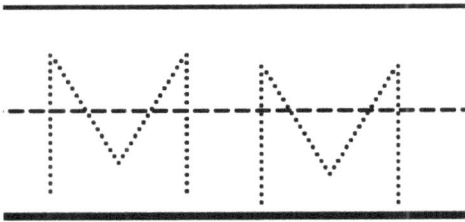

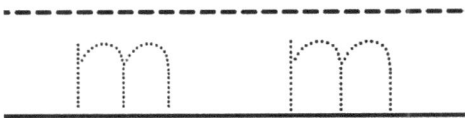

Find the Letters

Trace the letters. Then color the circles that have the letter you traced.

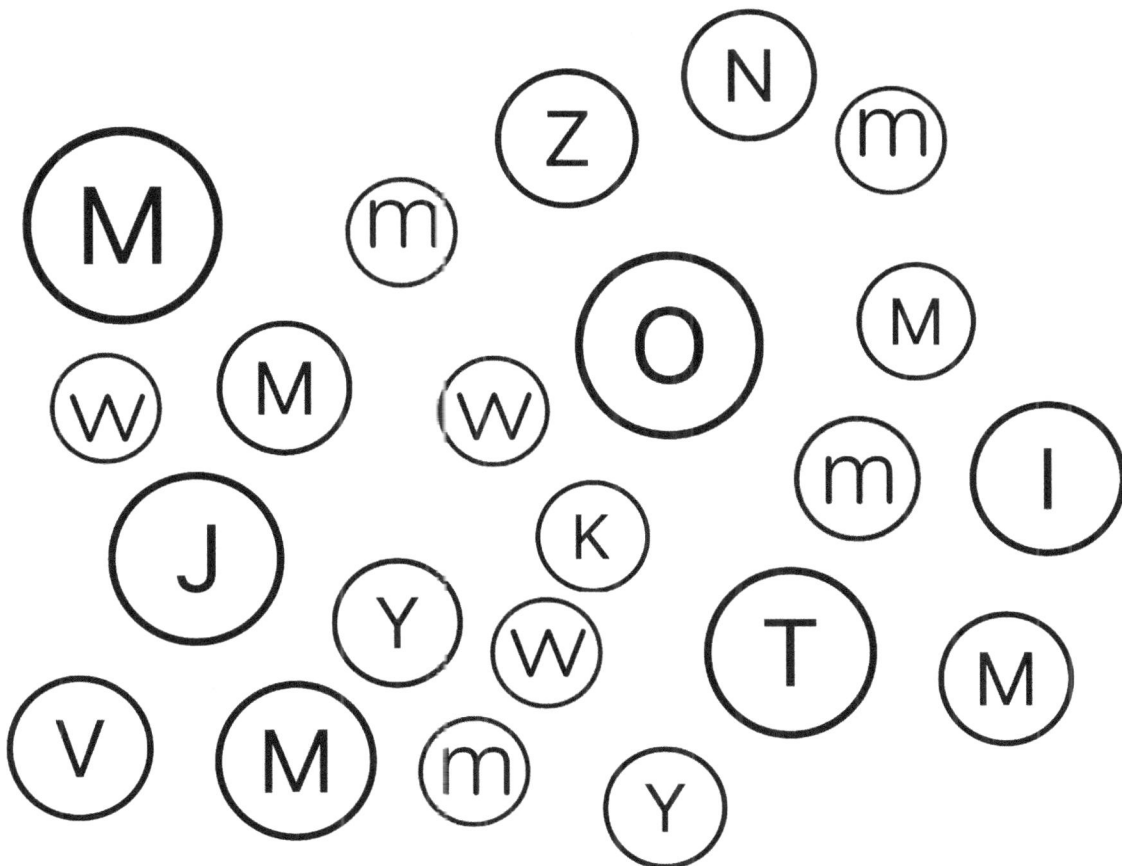

M M M

m m

Name: ....

N N N

n n

Find the letters

Trace the letters. Then color the circles that have the letter you traced.

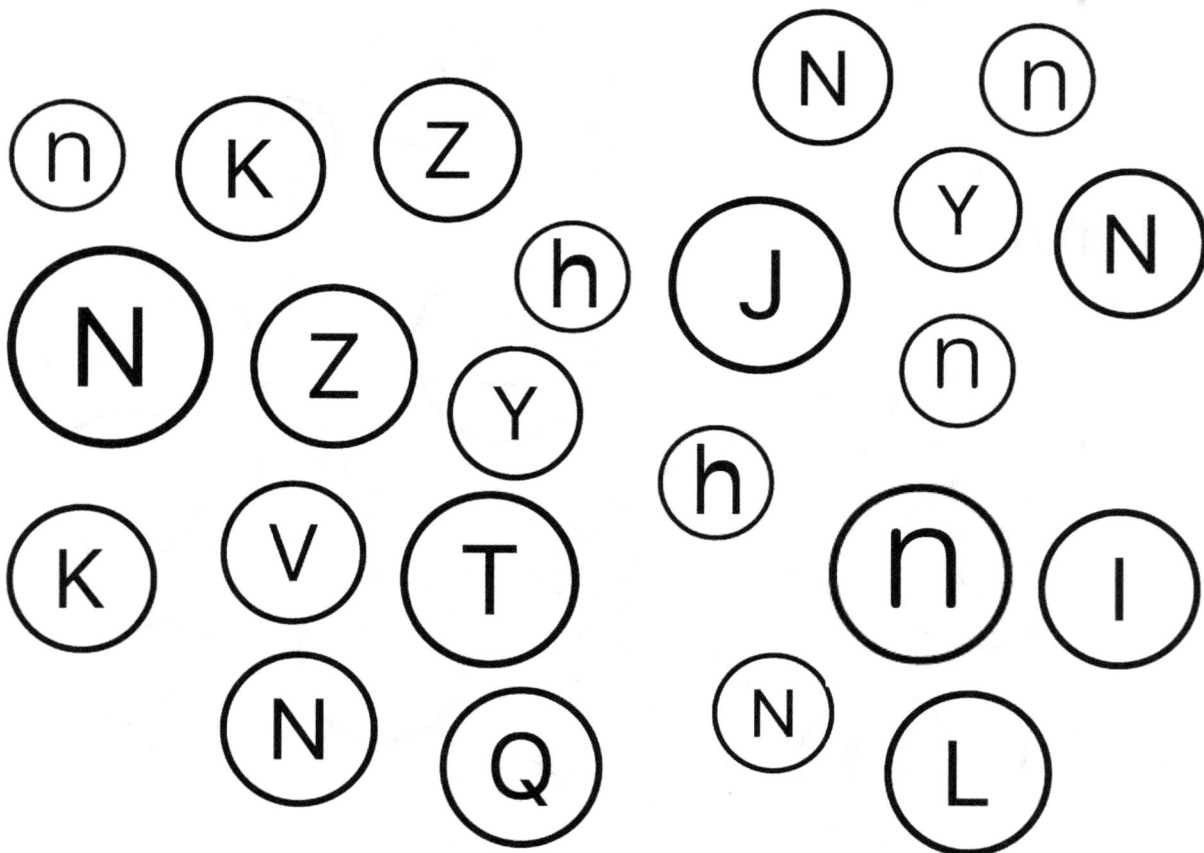

n K Z N n

N Z h J Y N

Y n

K V T h n I

N Q N L

Name: ....

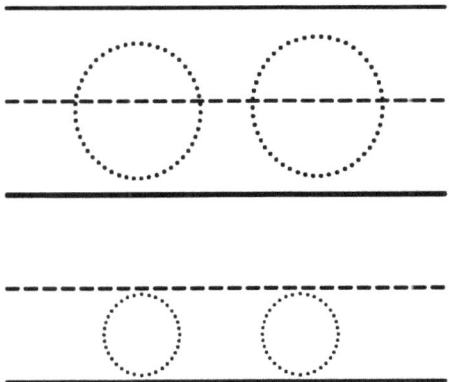

Find the Letters

Trace the letters. Then color the circles that have the letter you traced.

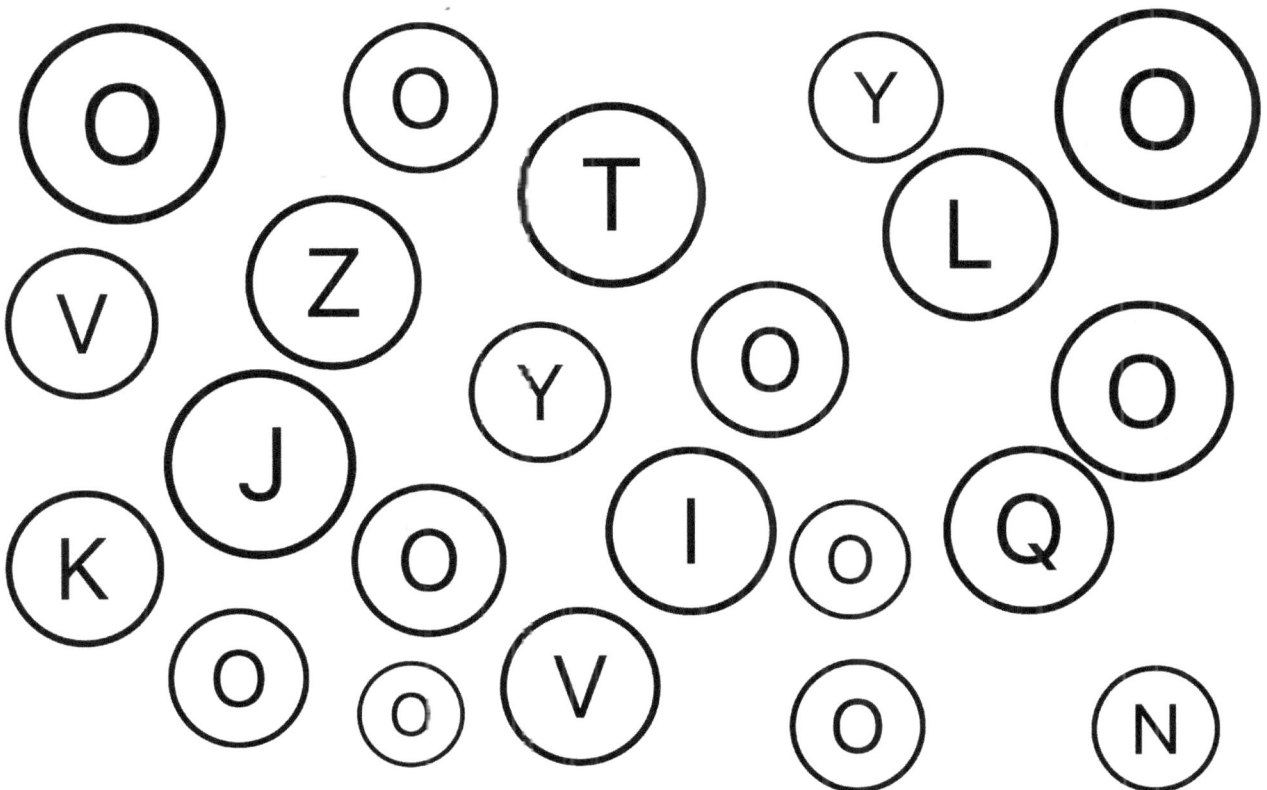

O O T Y O Z V L Y J O I O Q K O V O N

Name: ....

P P

p p

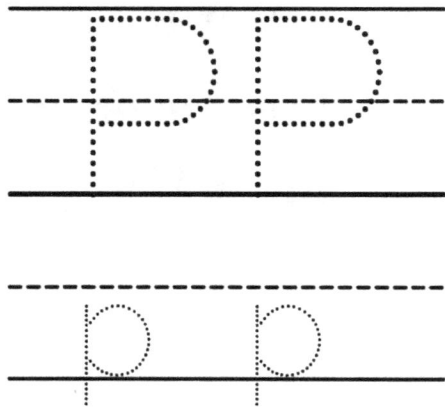

Find the letters

Trace the letters. Then color the circles that have the letter you traced.

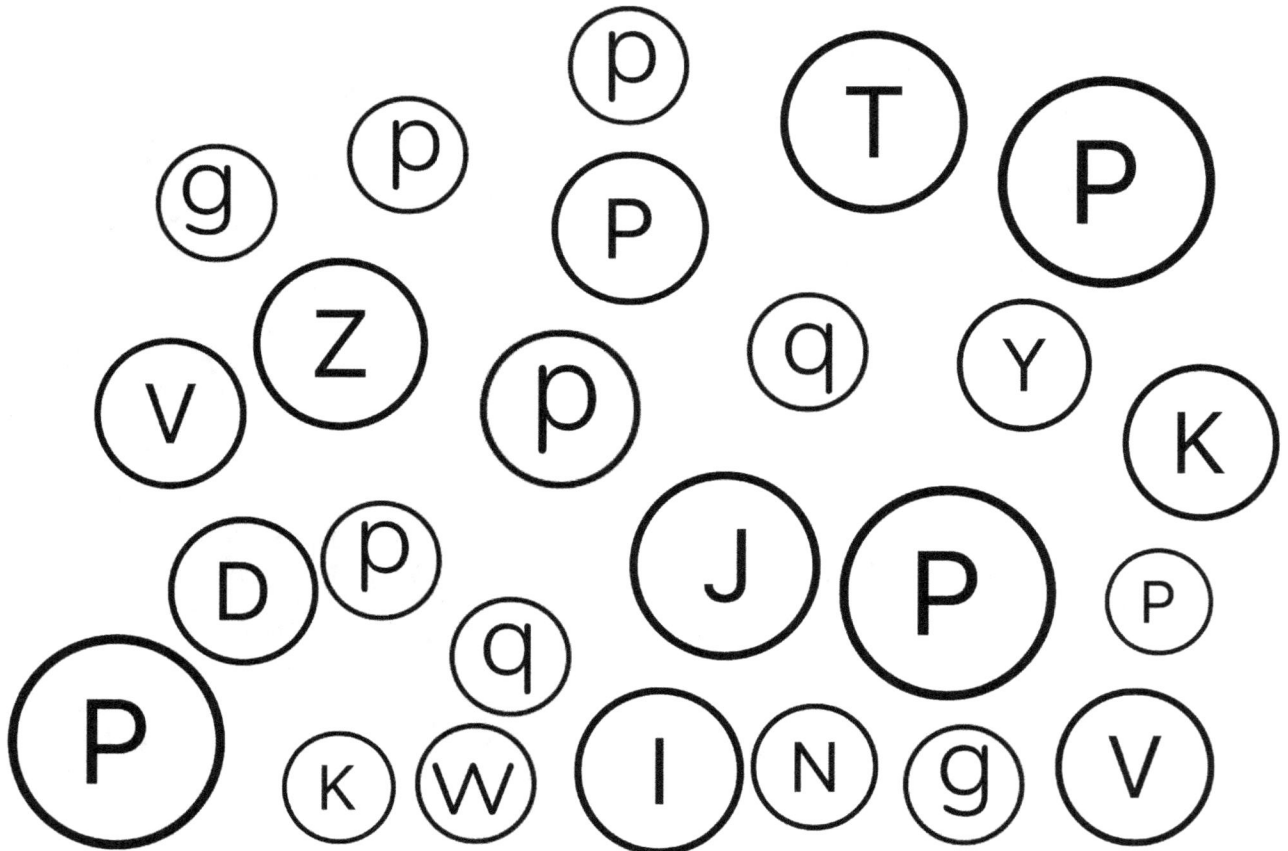

p
p
g
T
P
P
P
v
Z
q
Y
p
K
D
p
J
P
P
q
P
K
W
I
N
g
V

Name:

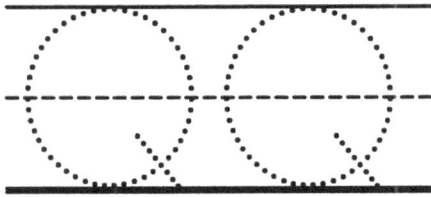

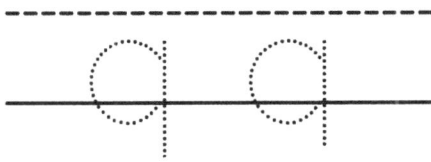

Find the Letters

Trace the letters. Then color the circles that have the letter you traced.

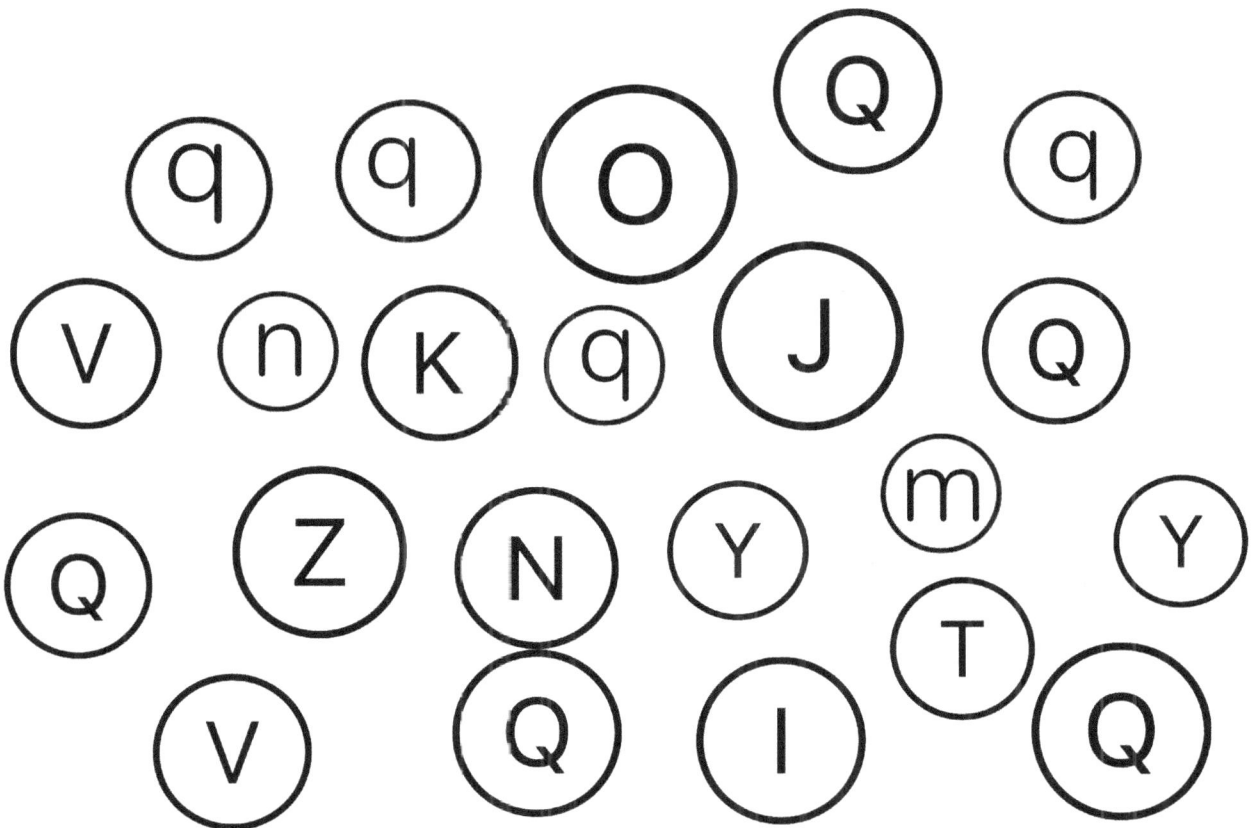

Q Q

q q

q q Q O Q q

v n K q J Q

Q Z N Y m Y

V Q I T Q

Name:

R R

r r

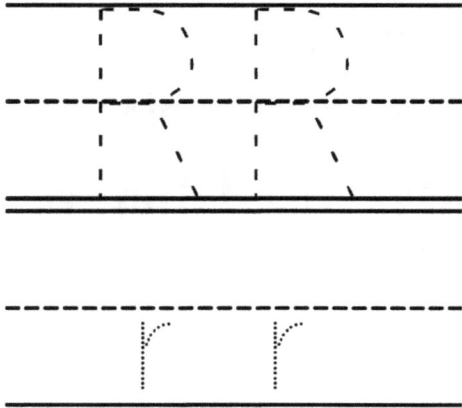

Find the letters

Trace the letters. Then color the circles that have the letter you traced.

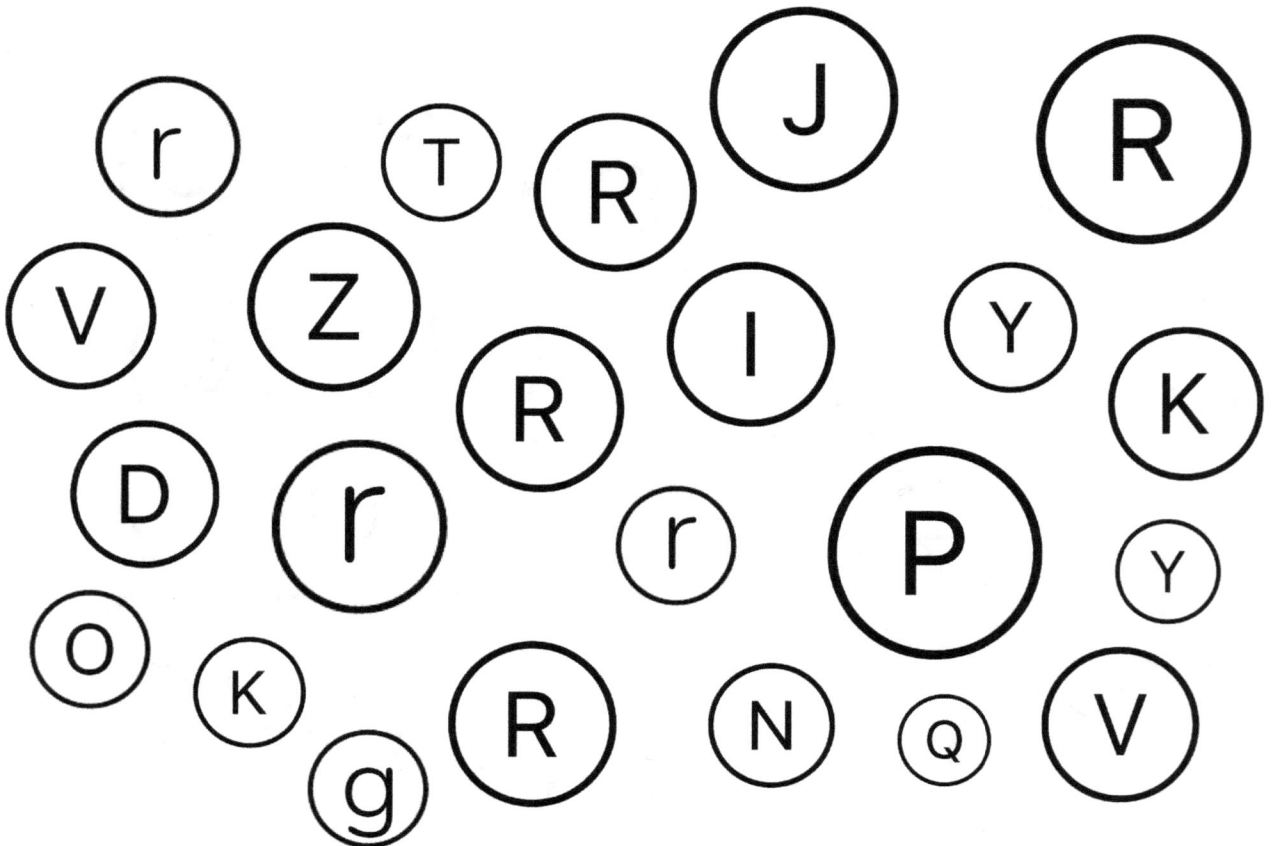

r   T   R   J   R

v   Z   R   I   Y   K

D   r   R   r   P   Y

o   k   R   N   Q   V
g

Name:

S S

s s

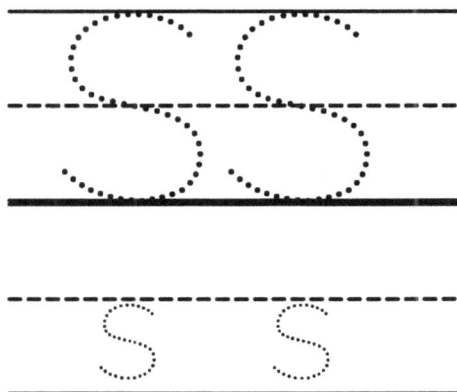

Find the Letters

Trace the letters. Then color the circles that have the letter you traced.

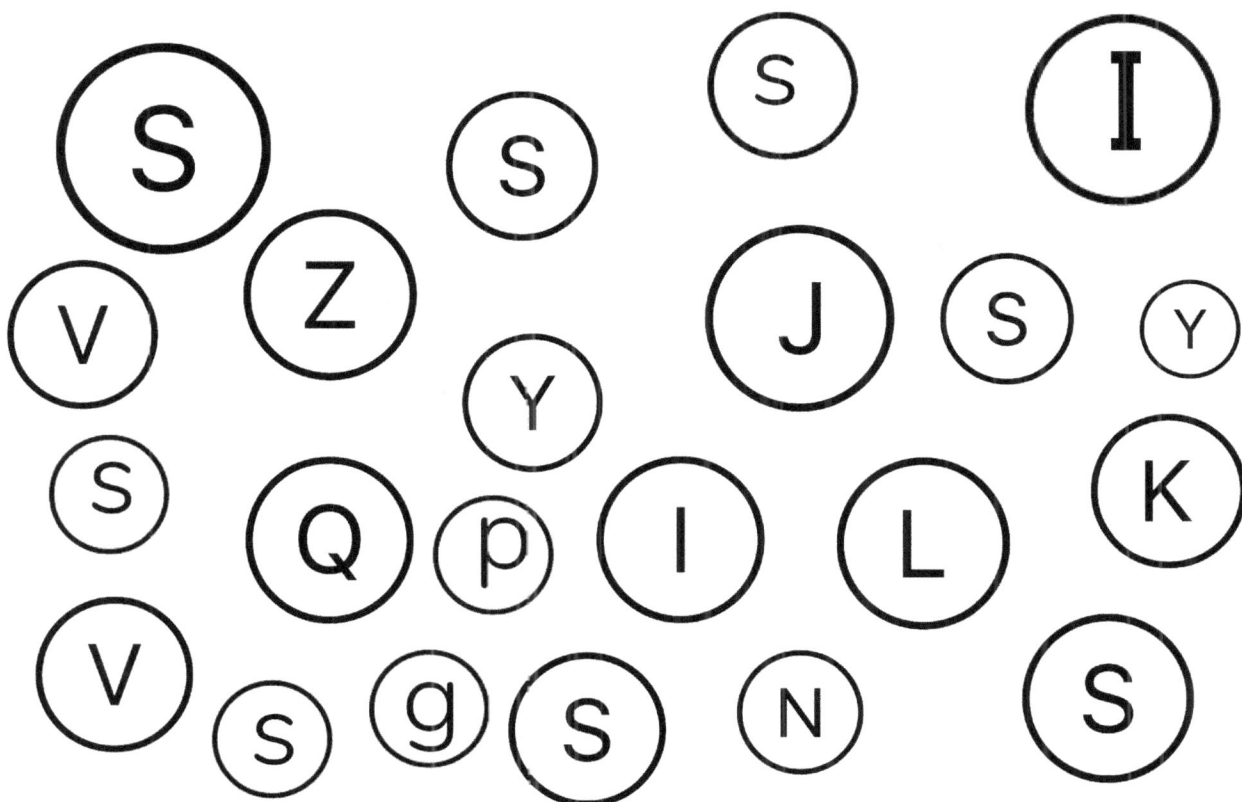

S s s I
v Z J S Y
s Y K
Q p I L
V s g S N S

Name: ....

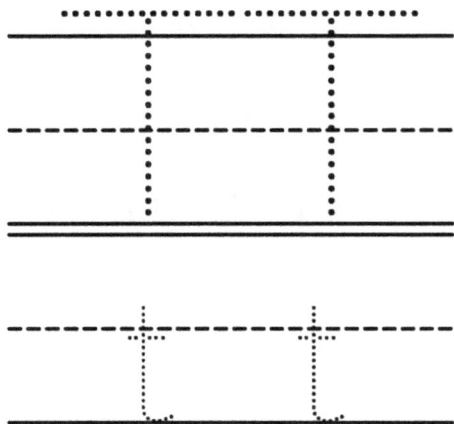

Find the letters

Trace the letters. Then color the circles that have the letter you traced.

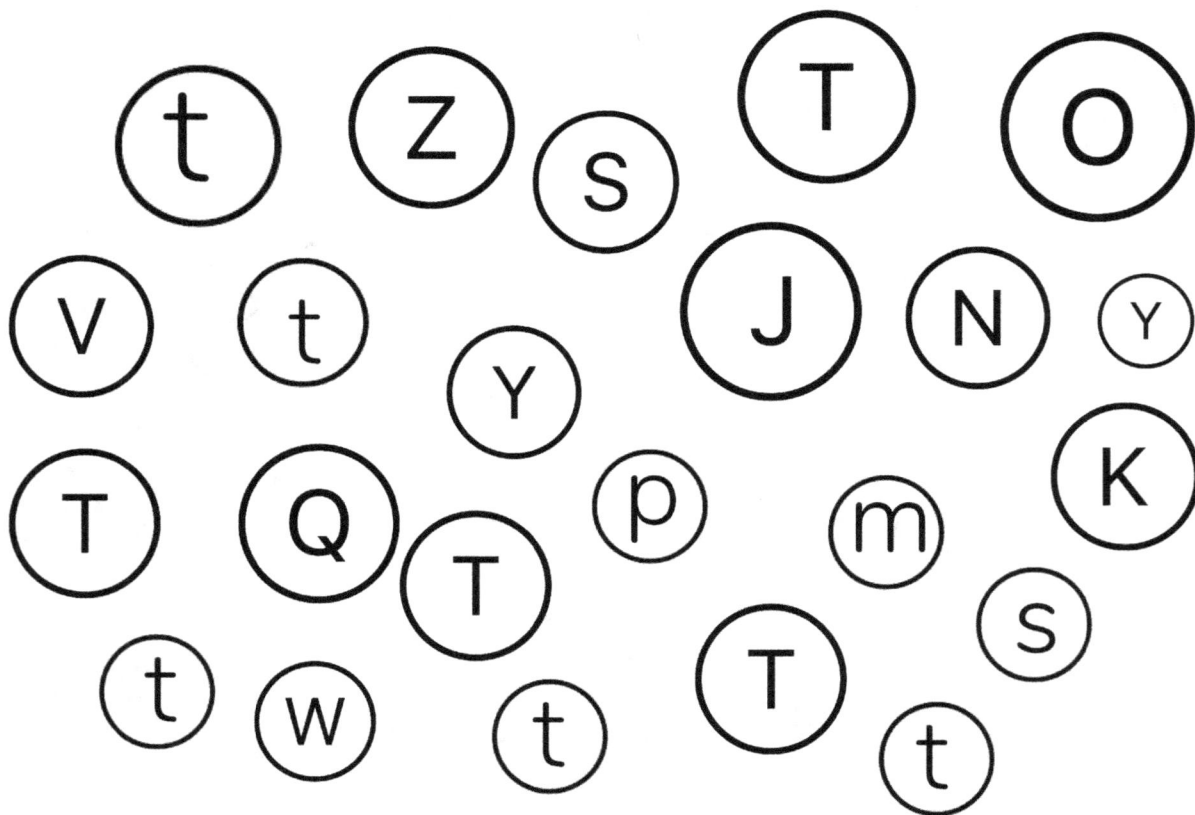

Name:

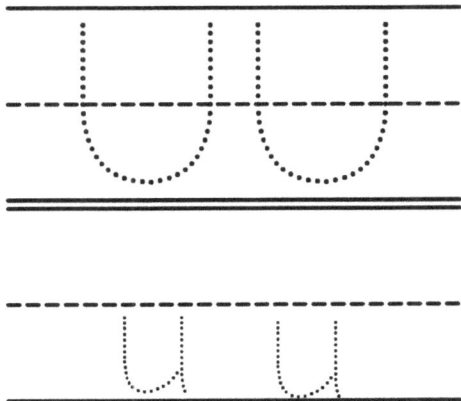

Find the Letters

Trace the letters. Then color the circles that have the letter you traced.

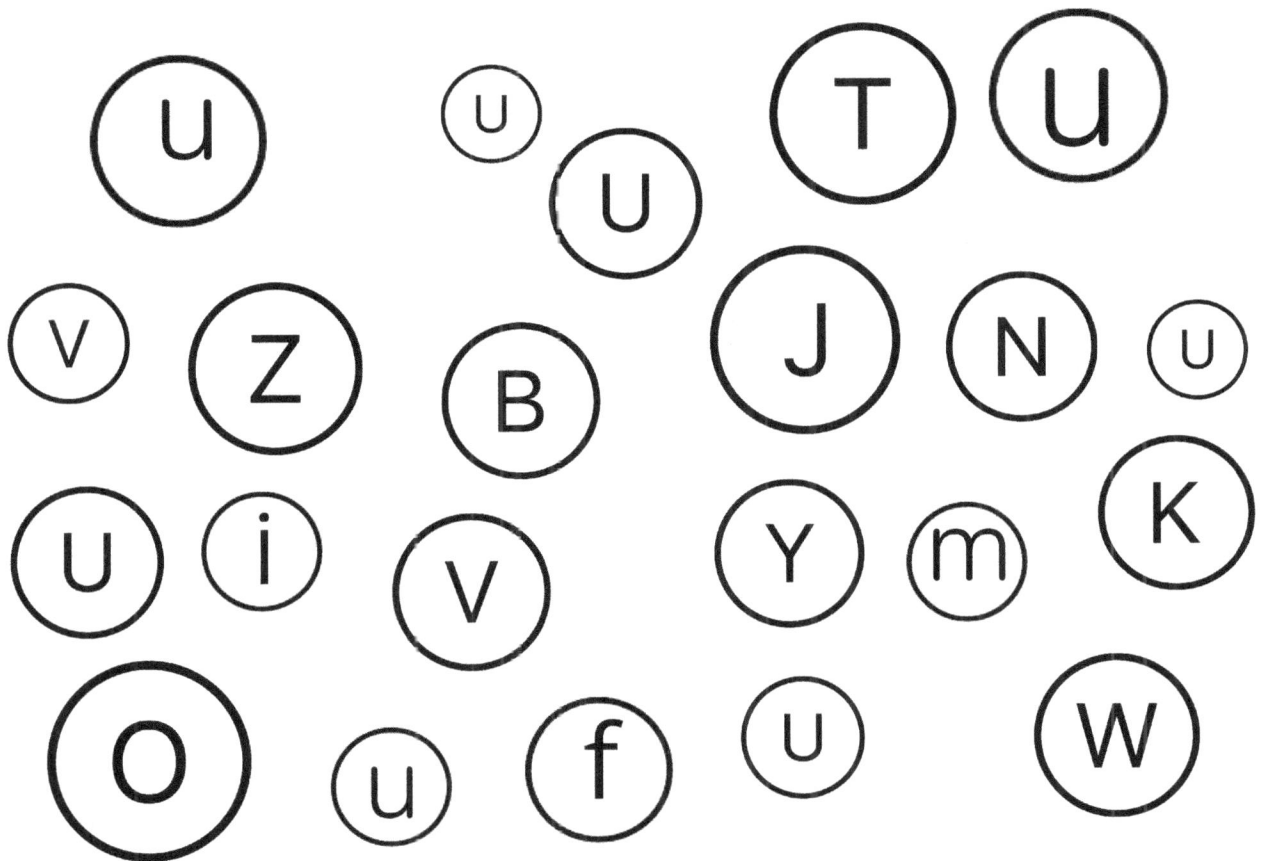

u u u T U

v Z B J N u

U i V Y m K

O u f u W

Name:

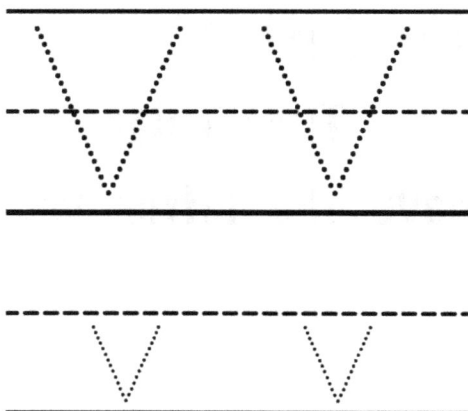

Find the letters

Trace the letters. Then color the circles that have the letter you traced.

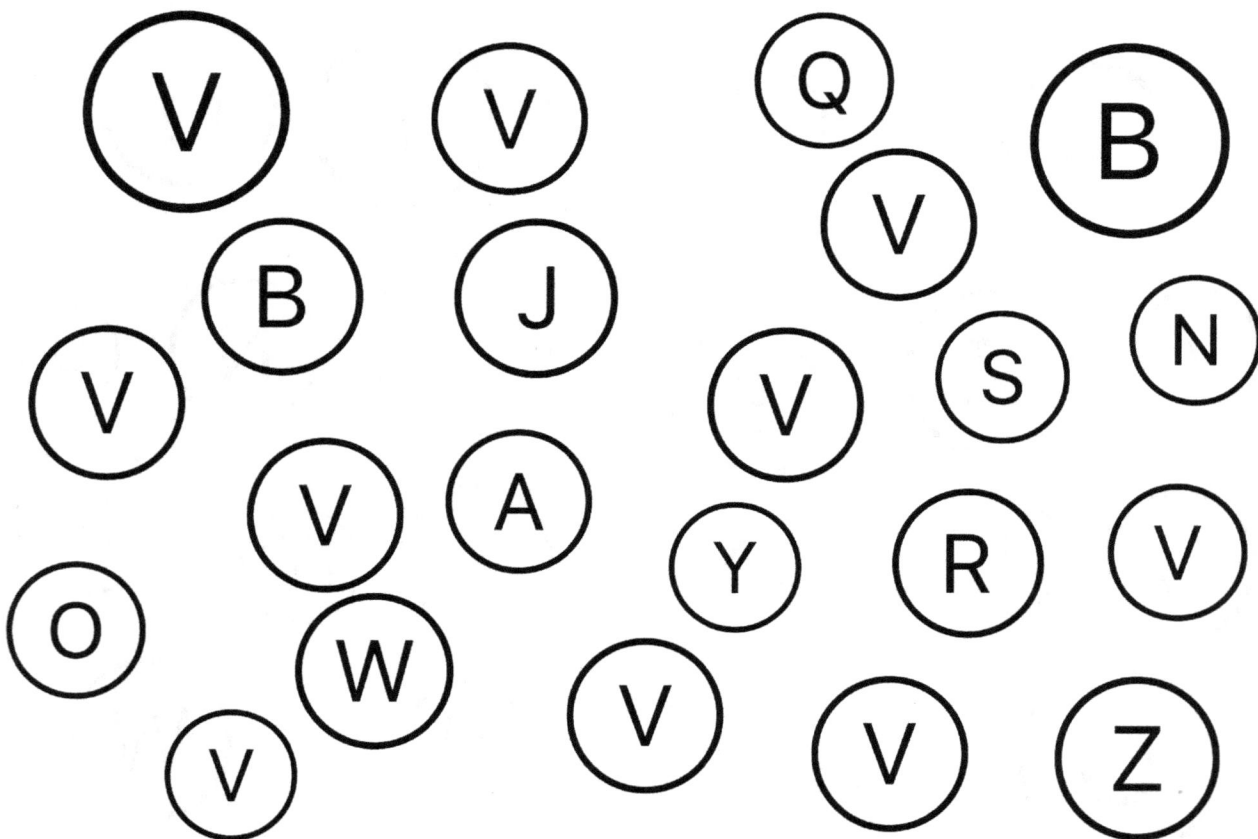

V V V

v v

(V) (V) (Q) (B)
(B) (J) (V)
(V) (V) (S) (N)
(V) (A) (Y) (R) (V)
(O) (W) (V) (V) (Z)
(V)

Name:

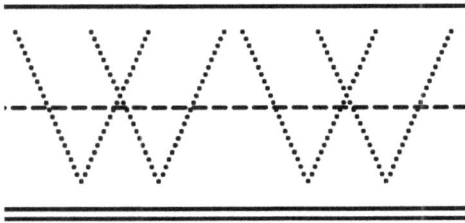

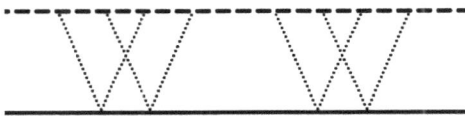

Find the Letters

Trace the letters. Then color the circles that have the letter you traced.

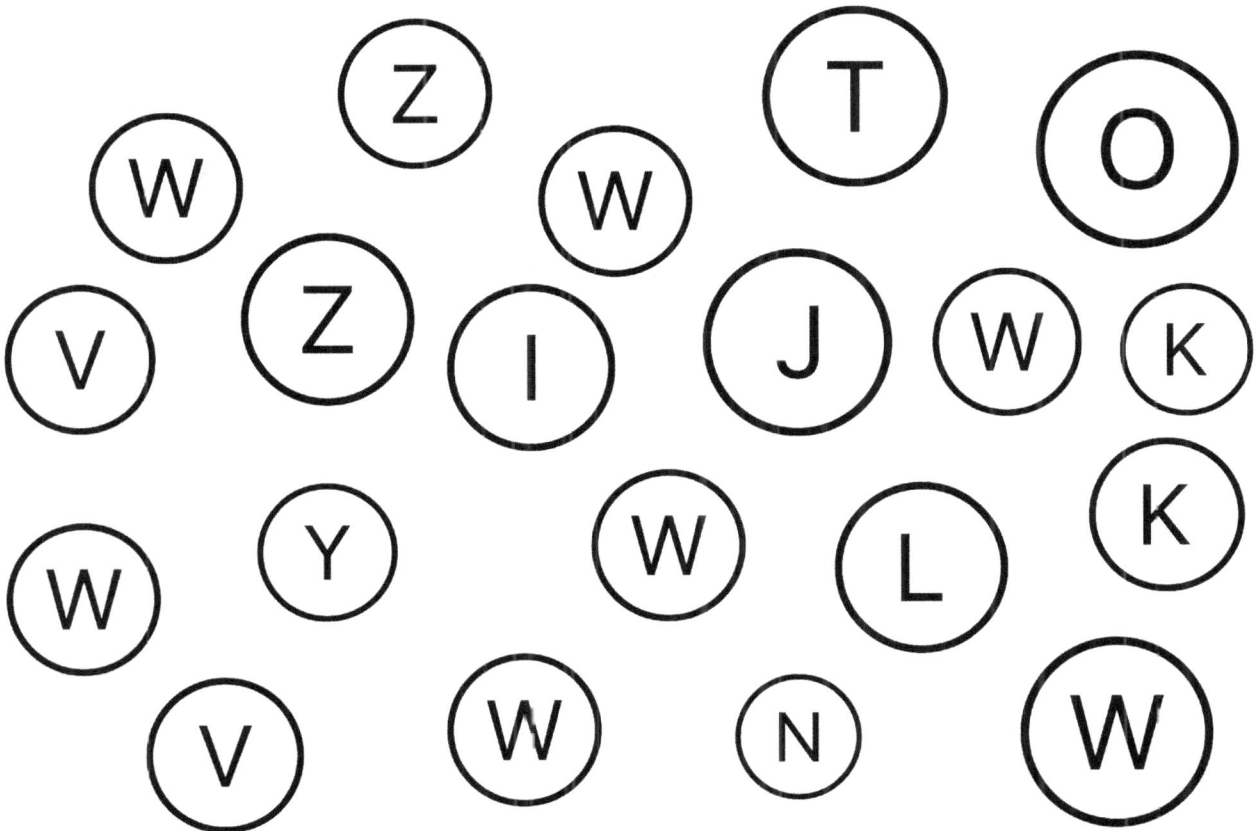

Z
W
T
O
V
Z
W
J
W
K
I
W
Y
W
L
K
W
V
W
N
W

Name:

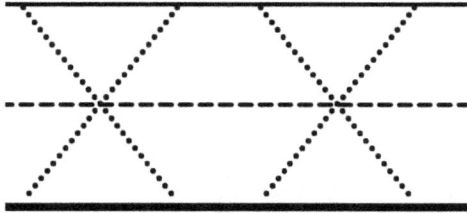

Find the letters

Trace the letters. Then color the circles that have the letter you traced.

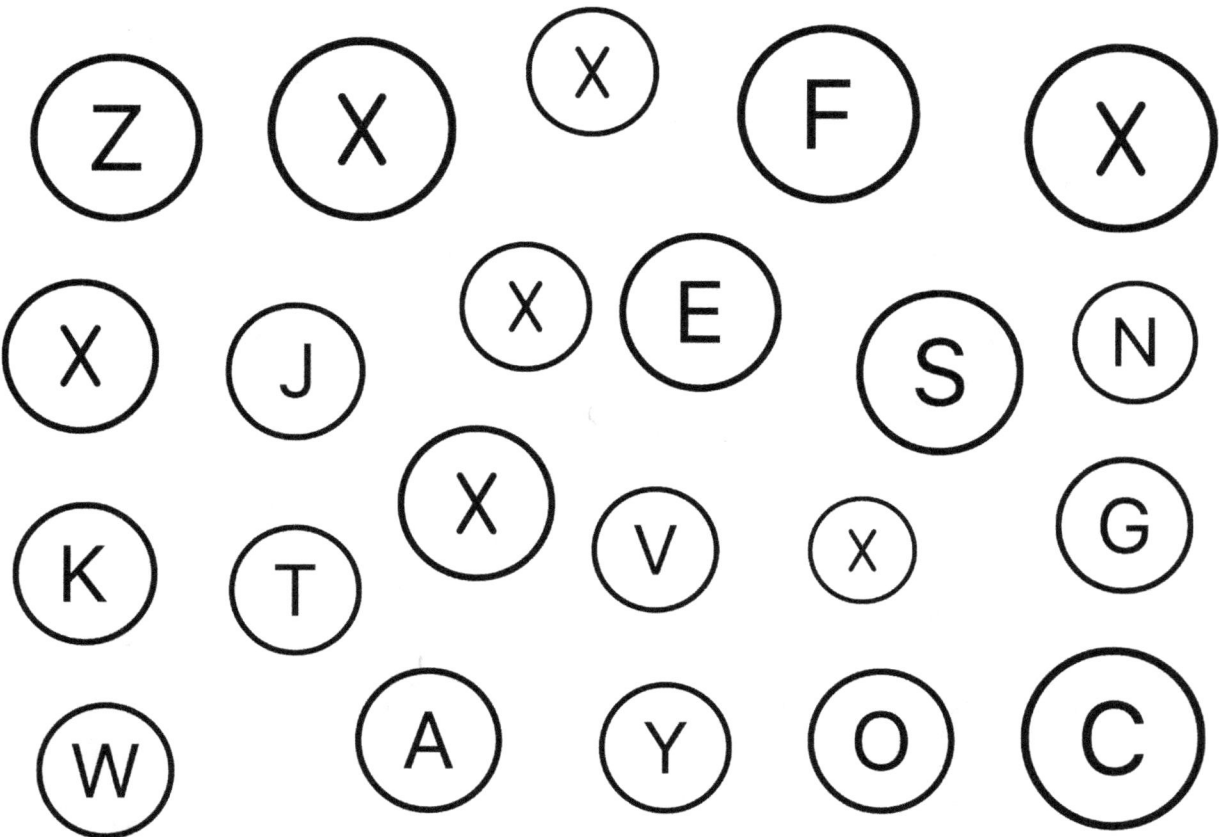

Z X X F X

X J X E S N

K T X V X G

W A Y O C

Name:

Y Y

y y

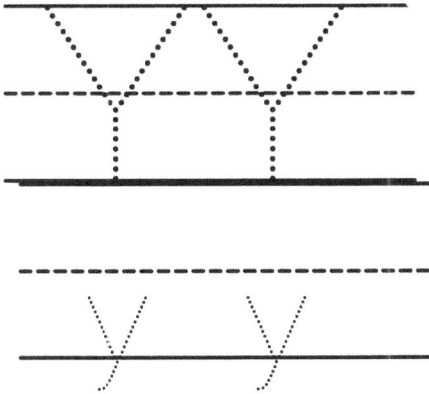

Find the Letters

Trace the letters. Then color the circles that have the letter you traced.

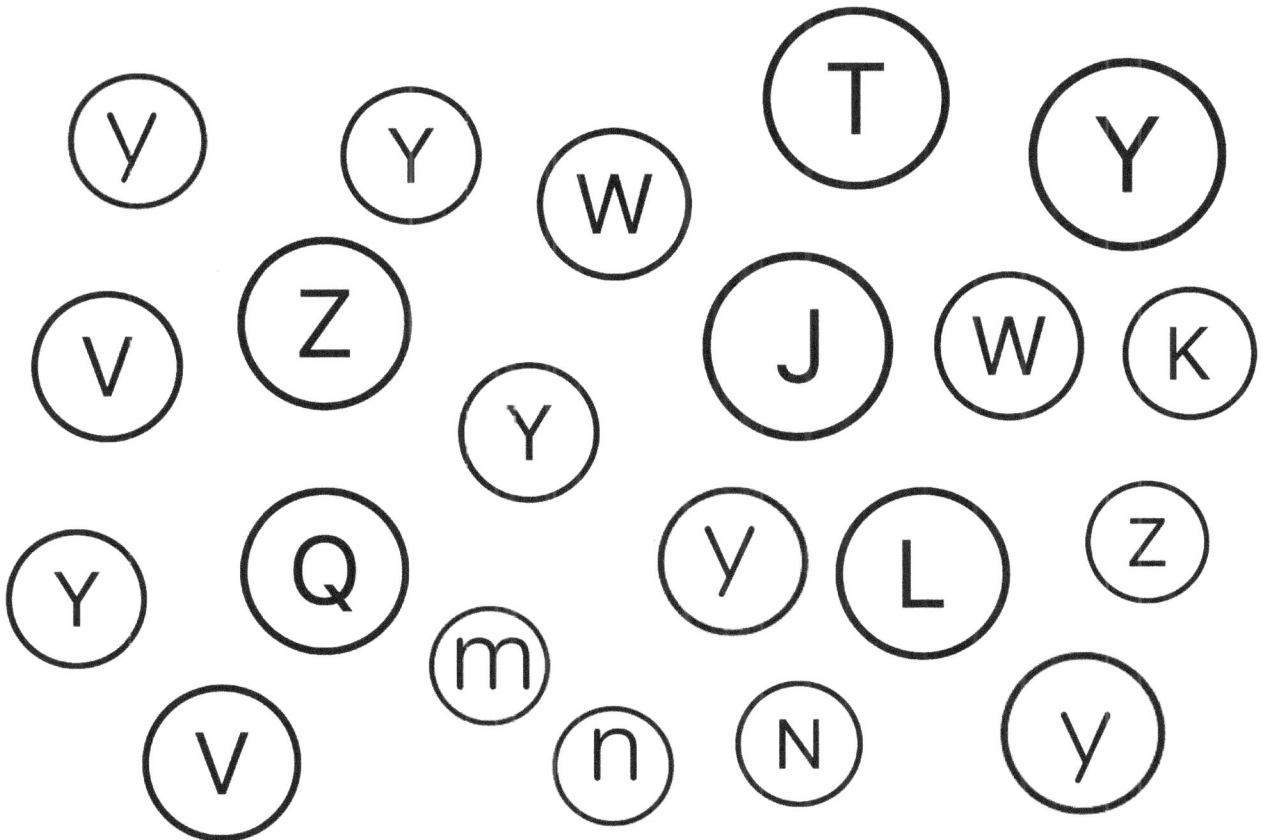

y Y W T Y

V Z J W K

Y

Y Q y L z

m

V n N Y

Name:

Zz

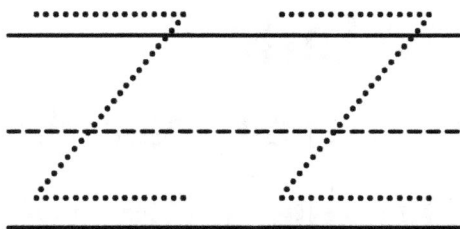

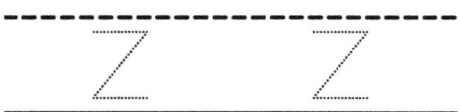

Find the letters

Trace the letters. Then color the circles that have the letter you traced.

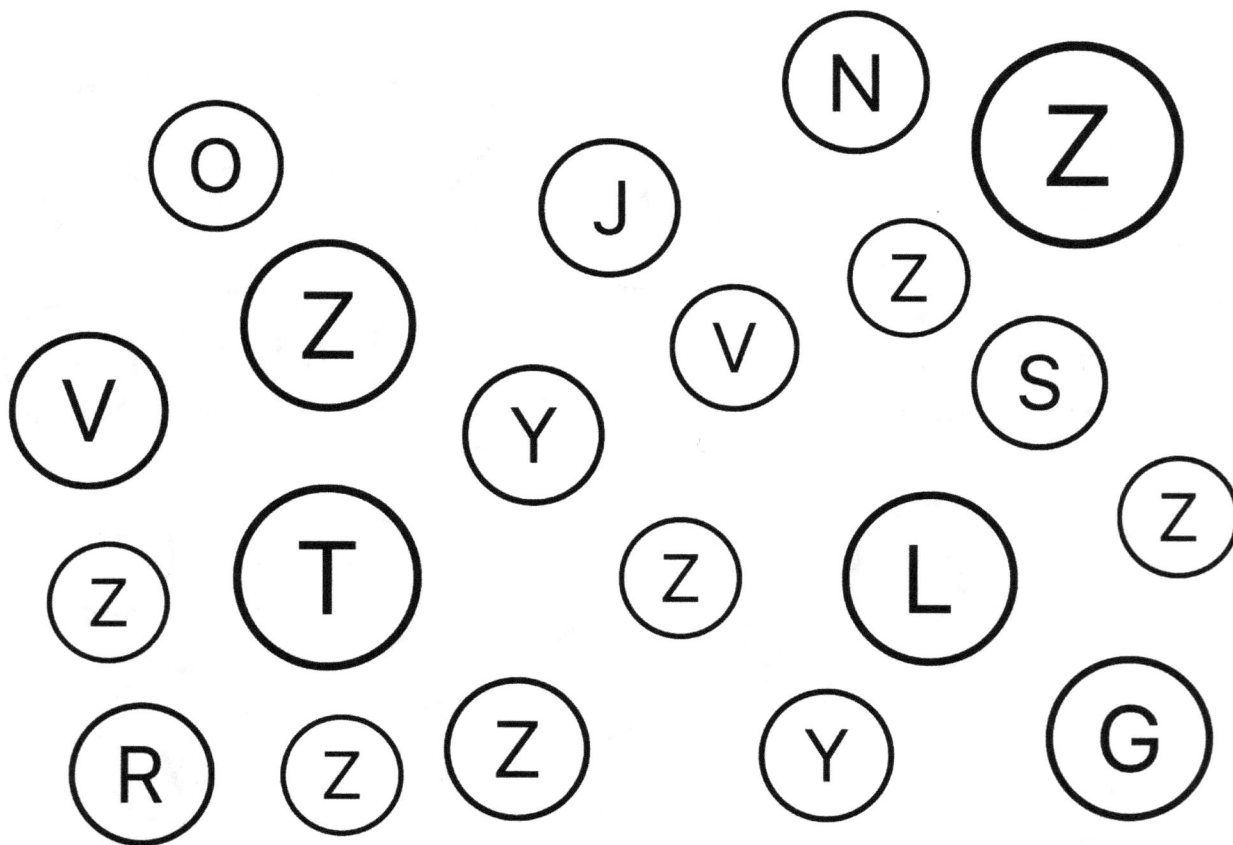

N

O   Z

J   Z

V   Z   V   S

Y

Z   T   Z   L   Z

R   Z   Z   Y   G

Name:

Trace the letters. Then write the letters at the bottom.

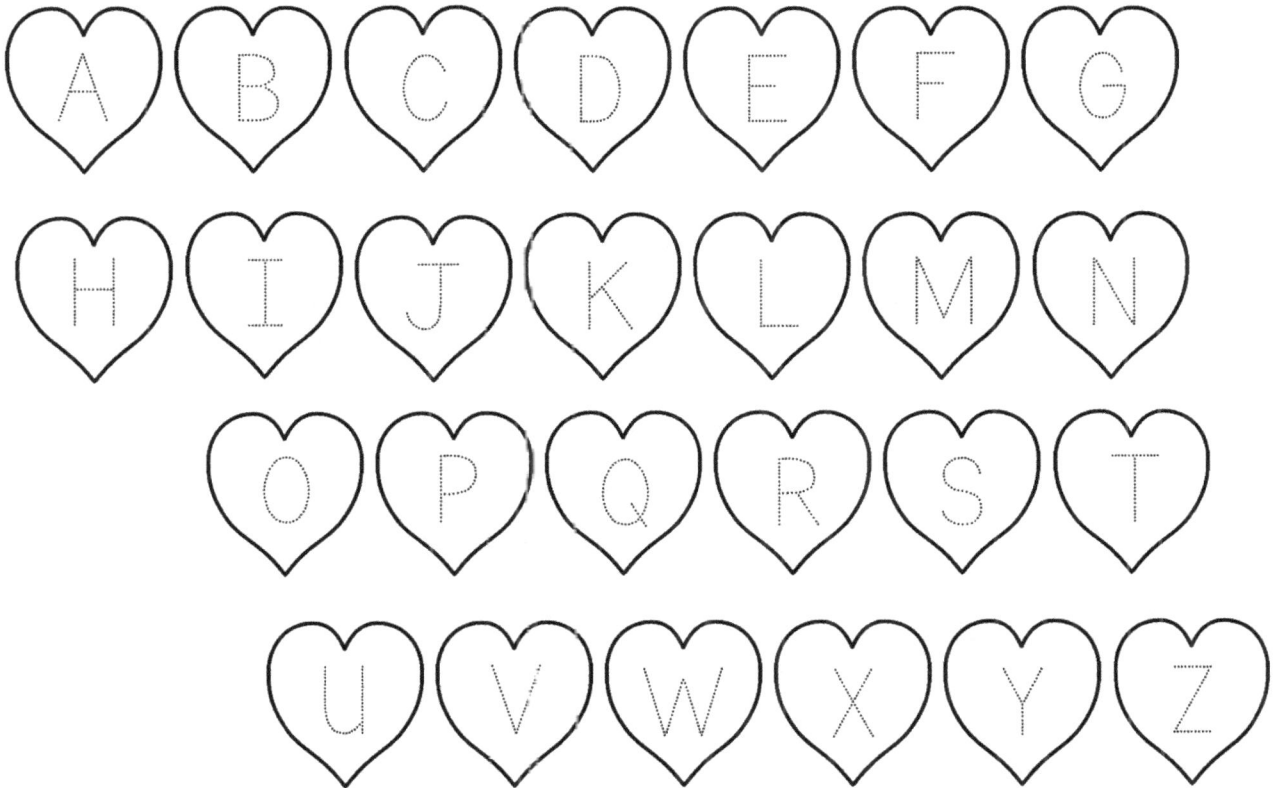

A B C D E F G

H I J K L M N

O P Q R S T

U V W X Y Z

Write your name with the first letter capitalized:

Connect the dots from A — Z

Connect the dots from A — Z

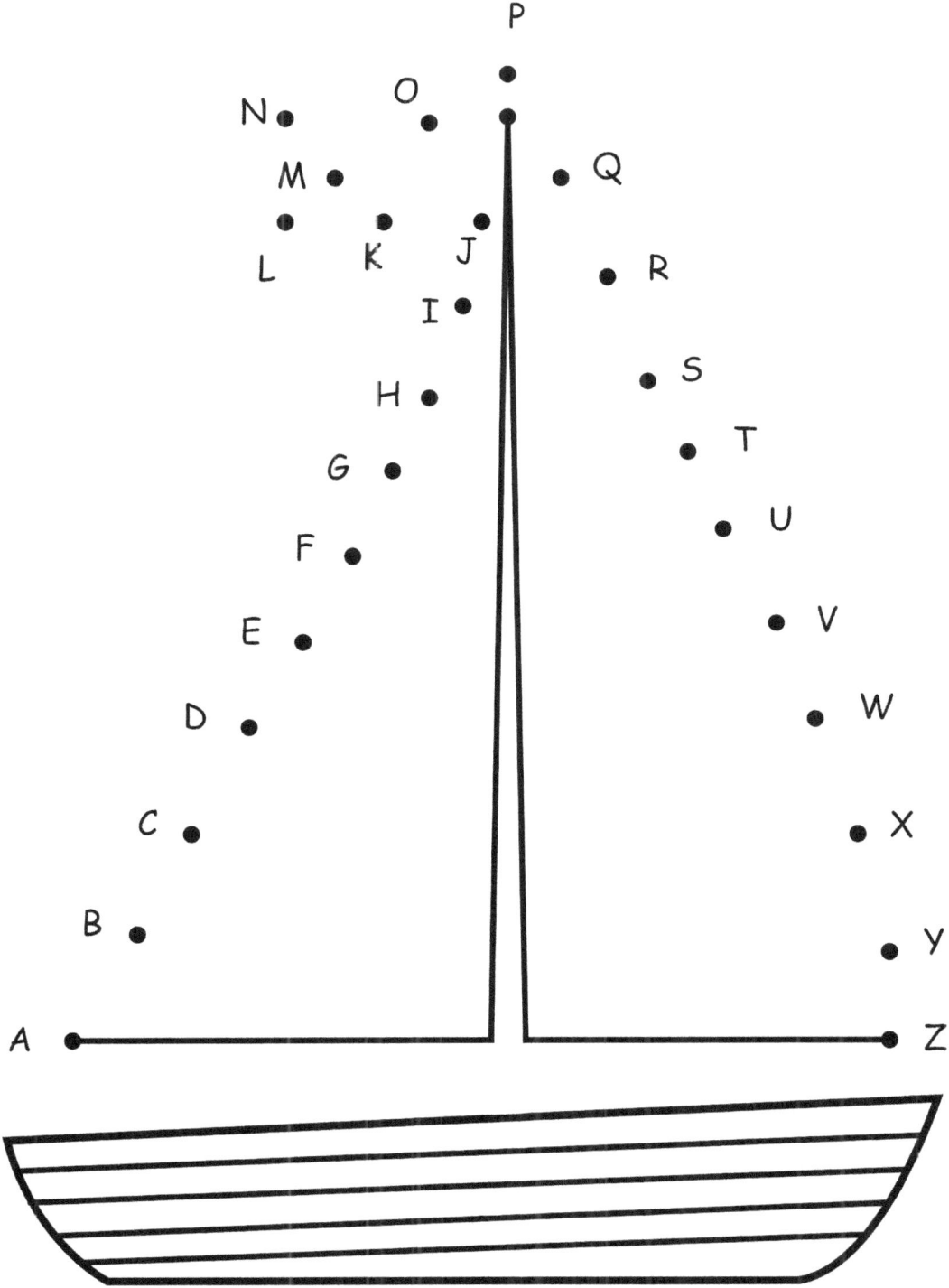

N O P
M Q
L K J R
I
H S
G T
F U
E V
D W
C X
B Y
A Z

Connect the dots from A — Z

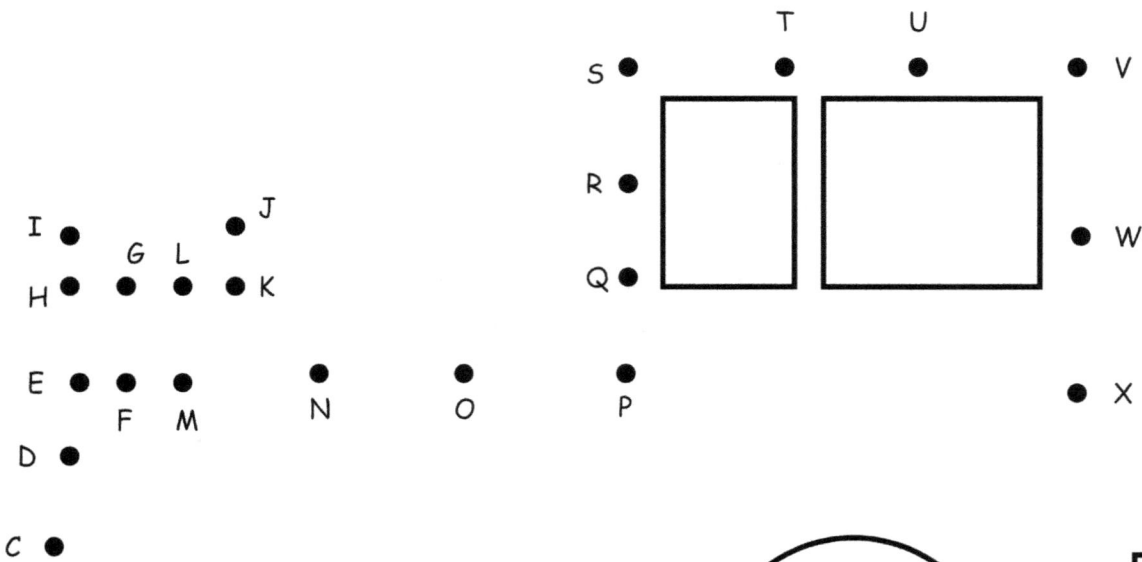

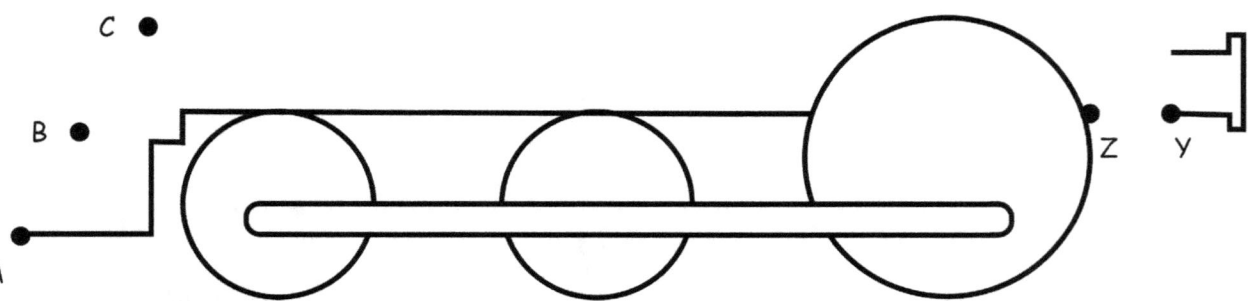

Connect the dots from A — Z

Exploring the Alphabet
Help the rocket discover the new planet by following the path from A to Z.

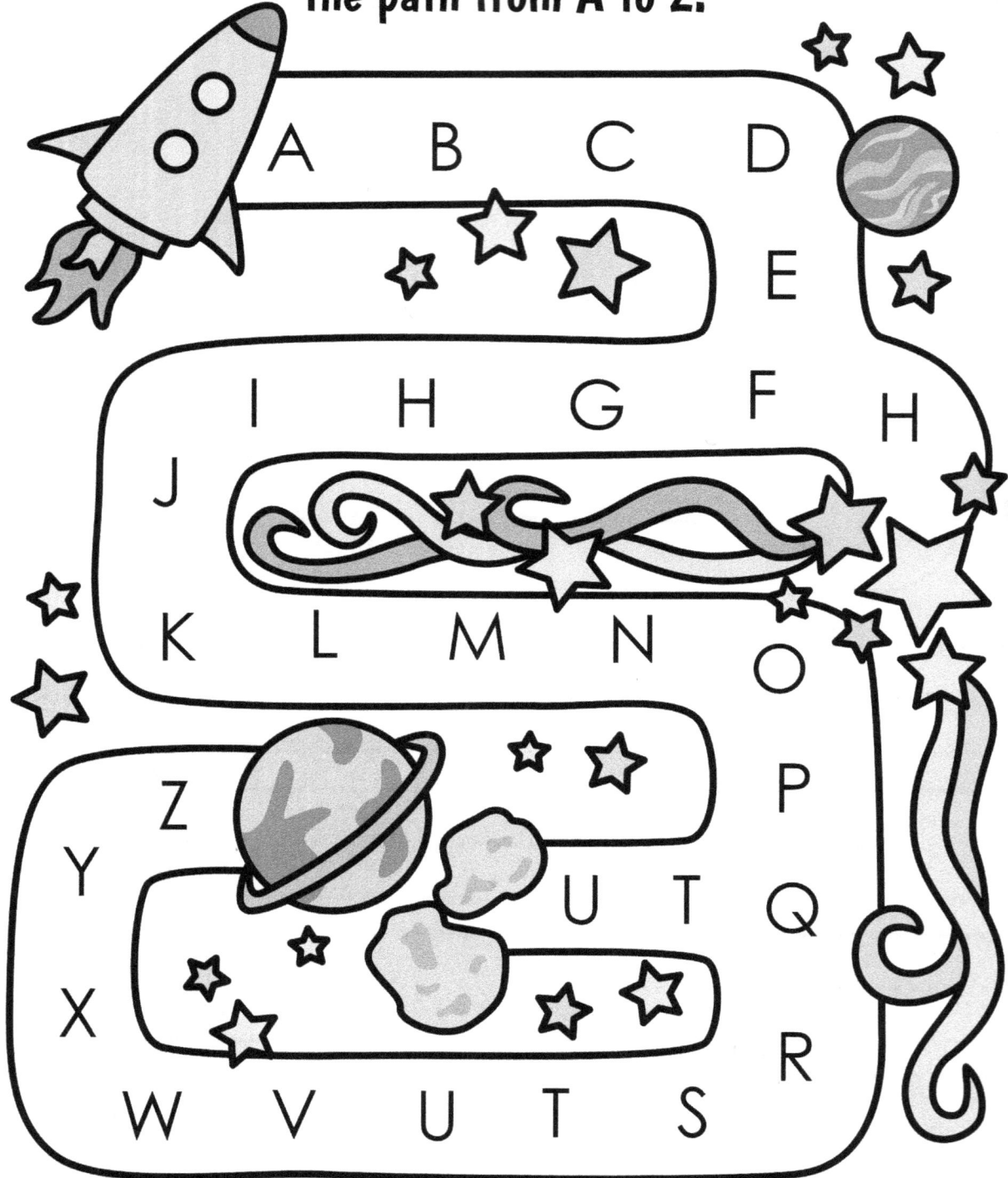

A   B   C   D

E

J   I   H   G   F   H

J

K   L   M   N   O

P

Z   U   T   Q

Y

X   R

W   V   U   T   S

More Alphabet Pratice

Circle all the uppercase letters and lowercase letters you find.
Write how many you counted.

Circle all the A's and a's.

B	I	o	A	A	a	o	p	n	m	o	a	e	r	g	y	a	z	c
G	y	a	a	d	q	p	A	B	P	X	Z	A	e	A	U	F	C	A

How many uppercase A's did you find? ☐ How many lowercase a's did you find? ☐

Circle all the B's and b's.

B	I	o	B	A	a	o	b	n	m	o	a	e	r	g	y	b	b	c
G	b	a	b	d	q	p	A	B	P	B	Z	A	e	A	U	F	C	b

How many uppercase B's did you find? ☐ How many lowercase b's did you find? ☐

Circle all the C's and c's.

S	I	o	C	A	a	c	b	n	m	C	a	c	r	g	y	C	b	c
G	c	a	b	C	q	p	A	B	P	C	Z	c	e	A	U	F	C	b

How many uppercase C's did you find? ☐ How many lowercase c's did you find? ☐

Circle all the D's and d's.

D	I	x	C	A	a	d	b	n	D	C	a	d	g	y	D	b	c	y
D	c	m	D	q	d	A	B	P	C	Z	w	d	A	D	F	C	b	s

How many uppercase D's did you finc? ☐ How many lowercase d's did you find? ☐

More Alphabet Pratice

Circle all the uppercase letters and lowercase letters you find. Write how many you counted.

Circle all the E's and e's.

E	v	o	C	E	a	d	b	w	D	E	a	d	e	u	D	e	c	c
D	c	e	D	q	S	E	B	e	C	Z	c	d	A	E	F	C	e	x

How many uppercase E's did you find? ☐ How many lowercase e's did you find? ☐

Circle all the F's and f's.

f	I	F	C	E	a	d	f	w	D	E	a	f	f	F	D	e	F	j
D	f	S	F	f	p	E	F	e	F	Z	c	d	O	E	F	f	e	y

How many uppercase F's did you find? ☐ How many lowercase f's did you find? ☐

Circle all the G's and g's.

G	g	I	S	C	G	a	d	g	G	D	G	a	f	g	H	D	e	F
X	f	G	g	M	g	G	F	e	F	Z	c	d	A	E	G	f	e	G

How many uppercase G's did you find? ☐ How many lowercase g's did you find? ☐

Circle all the H's and h's.

s	h	X	C	E	H	d	h	n	D	E	a	H	f	h	D	H	F	h
D	h	e	F	H	p	E	h	e	F	H	c	d	H	E	F	h	h	b

How many uppercase H's did you find? ☐ How many lowercase h's did you find? ☐

More Alphabet Pratice

Circle all the uppercase letters and lowercase letters you find.
Write how many you counted.

Circle all the I's and i's.

S	I	l	i	E	a	d	f	n	D	E	a	l	f	F	D	I	F	D
D	H	e	F	I	p	E	F	e	i	Z	c	d	A	E	F	f	I	H

How many uppercase I's did you find? ☐   How many lowercase i's did you find? ☐

Circle all the J's and j's.

s	J	j	F	C	j	a	m	f	n	J	E	a	J	f	J	D	j	F
D	f	e	F	f	j	n	F	e	F	Z	c	d	A	s	J	f	e	o

How many uppercase J's did you find? ☐   How many lowercase j's did you find? ☐

Circle all the K's and k's.

f	k	H	C	K	a	d	f	n	k	E	S	f	f	F	K	k	F
D	k	K	F	Z	K	E	F	K	k	Z	K	d	A	E	K	f	e

How many uppercase K's did you find? ☐   How many lowercase k's did you find? ☐

Circle all the L's and l's.

S	I	g	L	E	a	L	f	n	D	E	l	o	f	F	L	l	L	k
D	f	l	w	L	p	l	F	e	F	L	R	d	A	E	b	l	e	s

How many uppercase L's did you find? ☐   How many lowercase l's did you find? ☐

More Alphabet Pratice

Circle all the uppercase letters and lowercase letters you find. Write how many you counted.

Circle all the M's and m's.

f	M	s	B	z	m	d	m	n	m	E	m	f	j	M	D	e	F	u
D	m	e	M	f	o	t	M	e	F	Z	s	d	A	M	F	f	e	p

How many uppercase M's did you find? ☐ How many lowercase m's did you find? ☐

Circle all the N's and n's.

R	N	F	N	N	a	n	f	w	D	E	a	f	f	F	D	e	N
D	s	x	F	f	s	n	F	e	F	n	k	d	A	E	F	f	e

How many uppercase N's did you find? ☐ How many lowercase n's did you find? ☐

Circle all the O's and o's.

R	I	o	C	E	O	d	f	n	O	o	o	f	f	F	O	o	F	x
D	O	e	F	f	o	S	O	e	F	Z	c	d	A	K	o	f	e	w

How many uppercase O's did you find? ☐ How many lowercase o's did you find? ☐

Circle all the P's and p's.

P	I	p	C	P	a	p	f	P	D	P	a	P	P	F	P	e	F	P
G	P	P	F	f	p	P	F	P	F	Z	P	d	A	P	F	f	e	P

How many uppercase P's did you find? ☐ How many lowercase p's did you find? ☐

More Alphabet Pratice

Circle all the uppercase letters and lowercase letters you find. Write how many you counted.

Circle all the Q's and q's.

q	u	s	H	E	a	d	f	Q	D	E	a	f	Q	F	D	e	I	v
D	f	Q	q	Y	p	E	F	q	F	Z	c	Q	Q	E	F	f	e	Q

How many uppercase Q's did you find? ☐ How many lowercase q's did you find? ☐

Circle all the R's and r's.

d	R	v	r	E	a	r	f	R	D	Z	a	R	f	F	R	e	F	b
D	L	e	Y	R	p	E	r	e	F	Z	c	d	A	E	F	f	e	R

How many uppercase R's did you find? ☐ How many lowercase r's did you find? ☐

Circle all the S's and s's.

S	I	s	C	E	a	d	f	S	D	E	a	S	b	s	S	e	F	n
S	S	e	T	x	w	E	w	e	S	Z	s	o	A	E	F	f	e	s

How many uppercase S's did you find? ☐ How many lowercase s's did you find? ☐

Circle all the T's and t's.

w	I	Q	T	t	T	T	T	n	D	E	a	t	s	F	D	e	T	t
D	f	t	F	f	t	E	t	e	T	Z	c	T	A	E	G	f	e	p

How many uppercase T's did you find? ☐ How many lowercase t's did you find? ☐

More Alphabet Pratice

Circle all the uppercase letters and lowercase letters you find. Write how many you counted.

Circle all the U's and u's.

m	I	U	C	U	a	d	u	n	D	E	a	u	x	F	U	e	F	k
D	U	z	s	f	u	E	u	e	M	Z	c	d	u	R	F	f	e	w

How many uppercase U's did you find? ☐   How many lowercase u's did you find? ☐

Circle all the V's and v's.

f	I	V	V	S	a	d	S	n	D	E	N	v	f	F	v	e	F	s
v	f	v	F	f	p	V	F	e	F	V	O	v	A	V	F	f	e	j

How many uppercase V's did you find? ☐   How many lowercase v's did you find? ☐

Circle all the W's and w's.

A	I	W	C	W	x	d	w	n	D	w	a	o	W	w	D	e	F	b
t	w	e	w	f	p	s	F	e	W	Z	W	d	A	E	F	f	e	W

How many uppercase W's did you find? ☐   How many lowercase w's did you find? ☐

Circle all the X's and x's.

h	I	X	H	E	a	x	x	n	D	E	a	f	f	F	D	f	F	s
D	x	e	F	f	p	X	F	e	F	Z	X	s	A	E	X	f	e	X

How many uppercase X's did you find? ☐   How many lowercase x's did you find? ☐

More Alphabet Pratice

Circle all the uppercase letters and lowercase letters you find.
Write how many you counted.

Circle all the Y's and y's.

Y	I	d	C	y	M	Y	f	n	D	y	a	f	f	K	D	e	F	Y
D	f	e	y	Y	p	E	F	e	F	Z	Y	d	y	Y	F	f	e	p

How many uppercase Y's did you find? [ ]   How many lowercase y's did you find? [ ]

Circle all the Z's and z's.

Z	I	F	Z	E	m	d	Z	n	D	E	Z	S	A	Z	D	e	F	m
D	z	e	Z	z	p	Z	F	e	F	Z	c	d	A	E	F	f	z	c

How many uppercase Z's did you find? [ ]   How many lowercase z's did you find? [ ]

My Brain is Strong!
I Did It!

Color your brain
your favorite color.

USE ME!

**Look at the pictures.
Write your spelling words.**

_____

_____

_____

_____

_____

_____

Look at the picture.
Write your spelling words.

Look at the picture.
Write your spelling words.

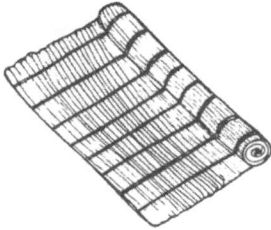

Look at the picture.
Write your spelling words.

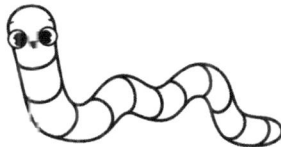

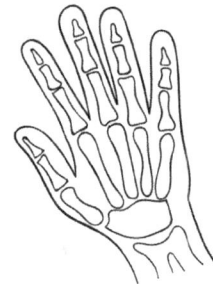

Look at the picture.
Write your spelling words.

_____   _____
- - - - - - - - -   - - - - - - - - -
_____   _____
_____   _____
- - - - - - - - -   - - - - - - - - -
_____   _____

Write your favorite spelling words.

_____   _____   _____
- - - - - - -   - - - - - - -   - - - - - - -
_____   _____   _____
_____   _____   _____
- - - - - - -   - - - - - - -   - - - - - - -
_____   _____   _____

Alphabet Sounds

PHONICS and READING

Phonics is matching the sounds of spoken English with individual letters or groups of letters. It is used to teach children the relationship between letters and the sounds that they make. Phonics is all about using sounds to read words.

Tap and blend

1. Using their workbook, first, let students tap out each individual sound in the word.
2. Then, students should blend the sounds to read the word smoothly. This is done as the student moves his or her finger on the arrow from left to right.
3. To help students build fluency, have students practice tapping the words a few times then ask them to blend the sounds without tapping first.

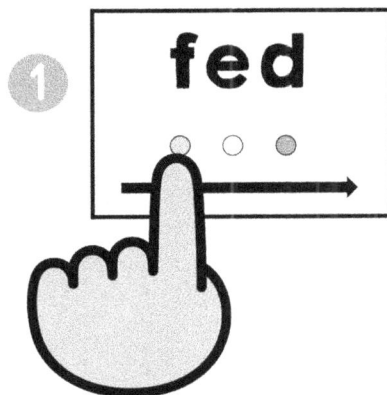

1 **fed**

2 **fed**

Tap each sound

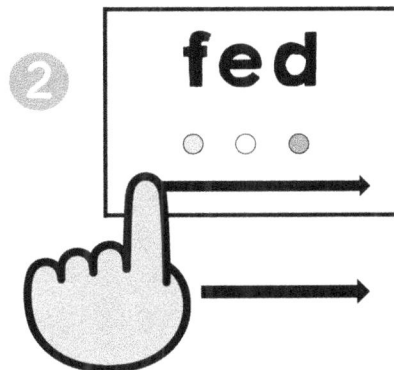

Blend the sounds to read the word.

Let's learn the sounds of the alphabet!

A   say /a/ as you can hear this in apple, ant, alligator.

B   say the sound /b/ as you can hear this in bat, balloon, baby.

C   say /c/ as in Car, Cap, Cub.

D   say /d/ as in Drum, Dog, Doll

E   try to break an imaginary egg in your hand and say /e/ As in Egg, Eggplant

F   say /f/ as in Fish, Frog

G   say /g/ as in Grapes, Gate

H   say /h/ as in Horse, Hat, Hen

I   say /i/ as in Inkpot, Igloo

J   say /j/ as in Jam, Jar

K   say /k/ as in Kettle, Kite

L   Put your finger in front of your mouth and roll your tongue behind your teeth and say /l/

M   say /m/ as in Mango, Moon

N   say /n/ as in Nose, Net

Let's learn the sounds of the alphabet!

O   say /O/ as in Orange, Octopus

P   Hold one finger in front of your mouth as it is a candle and blow slowly and say /p/ as in Pig, Pan

Q   say /qu/ as in Quack, Quilt, Queen

R   say /r/ as in Rat, Rabbit, Rain

S   say /S/ as in Socks, Six, Snail

T   say /t/ as in Tree, Tap, Top

U   say /u/ as in Up, Umbrella

V   Bite your lower lips and say /v/ and feel the vibration on your lips as in vet, van

W   Make a O with your lips like a kiss and blow it in your palm and say /W/ as in Watch, Web, Well

X   Take an imaginary camera and click and say /ks/ as in Fox, Wax, Box

Y   say /y/ as in Yak, Yawn, Yellow

Z   say /zzz/ as in Zebra, Zero, Zigzag

Beginning Sounds - What do you hear?

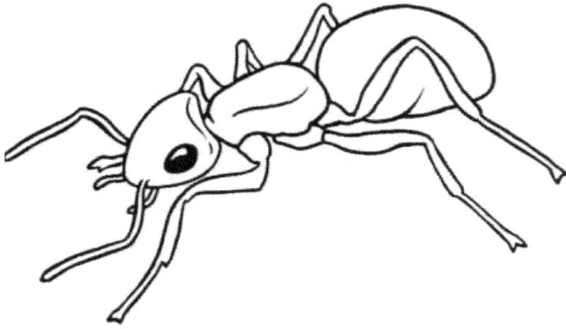

letter **A** sound - ant

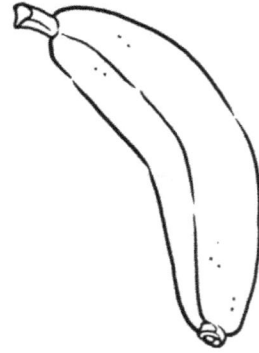

letter **B** sound - banana

letter **C** sound - cat

letter **D** sound - dog

letter **E** sound - elephant

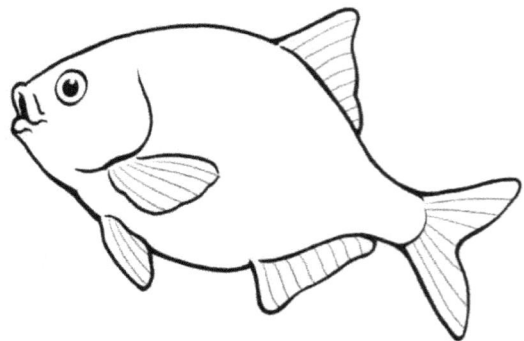

letter **F** sound - fish

letter G sound - goat

letter H - hat

letter I sound - ice cream

letter J sound - jacket

letter K sound - keys

letter L sound - lion

Color the square with pictures that begin with the /h/ sound to find the hidden letter.

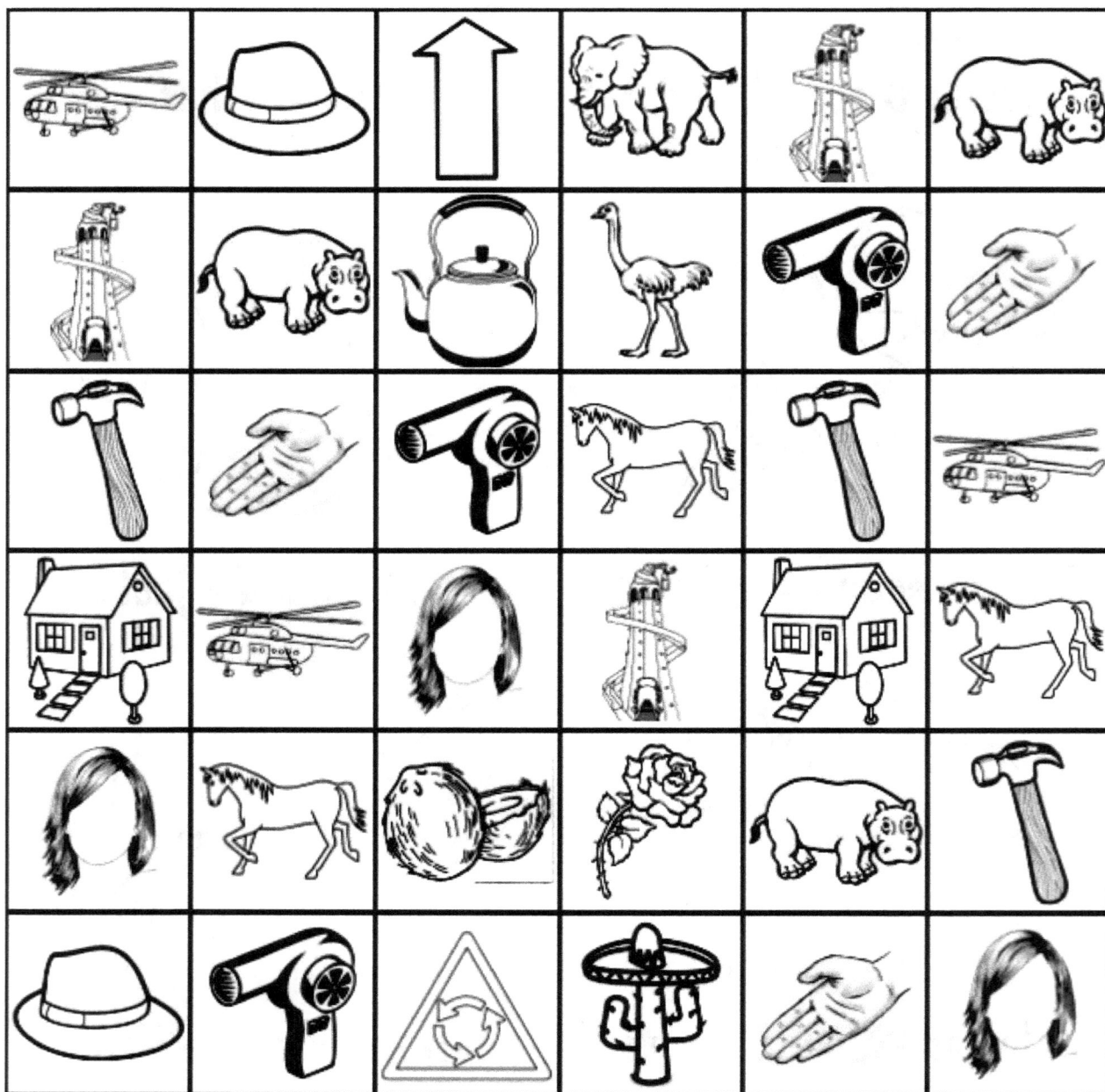

letter M sound - monkey

letter N sound - nest

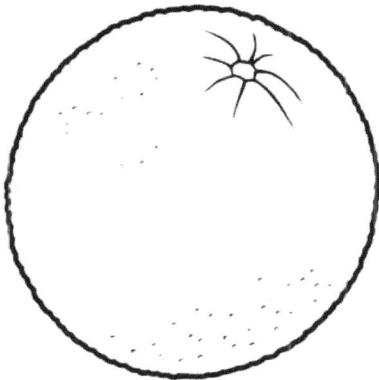

letter O sound - orange

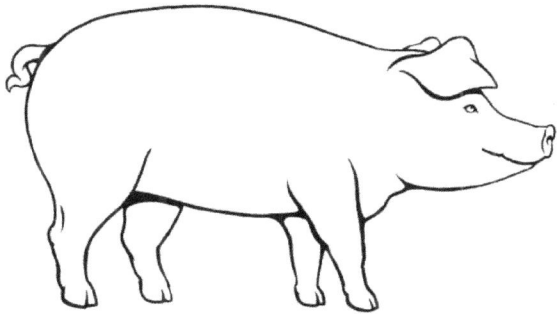

letter P sound - pig

letter Q sound - queen

letter R sound - rabbit

Trace uppercase M.
Color the pictures that begin with the /m/ sound.

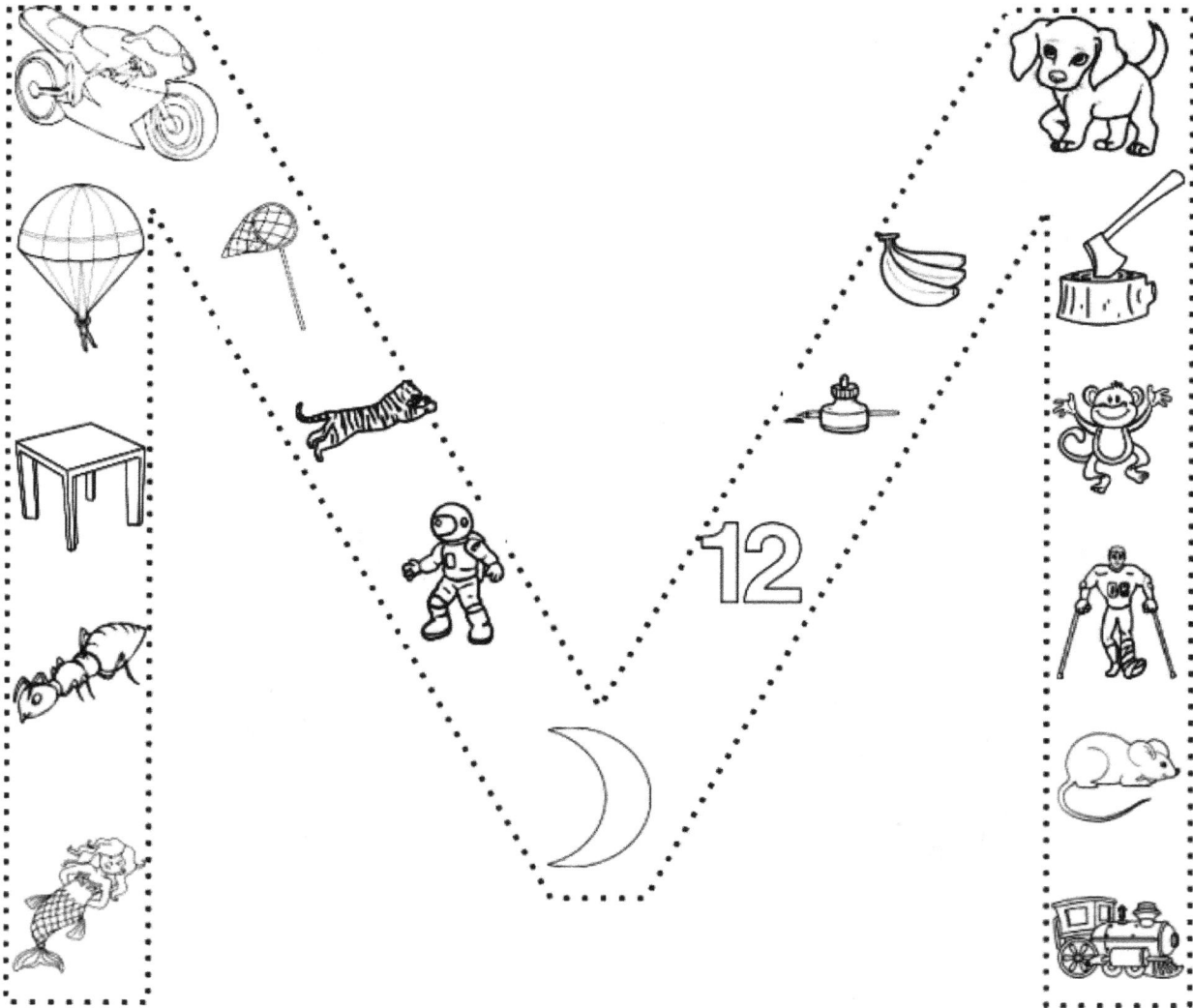

letter S sound - snail

letter T sound - table

letter U sound - umbrella

letter V sound - vest

letter W sound - watch

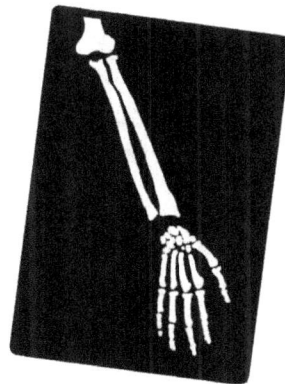

letter X sound - xray

Color the pictures that begin with the /t/ sound.
What is the hidden letter?

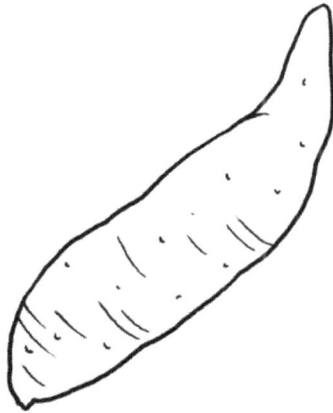

letter Y sound - yam

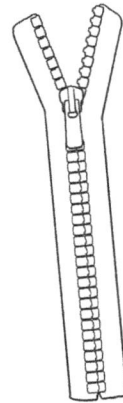

letter Z - zipper

Missing Vowels
Look at the pictures and fill in the missing vowel to complete each word.

m __ g   c __ t   b __ x

o	a	u

 10

r _ g   t _ _ n   v _ _ n

e	a	u

   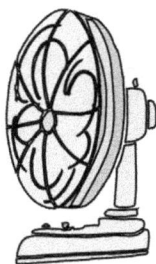   

k _ _ t   f _ _ n   b _ _ g

i	u	a

v __ n   l __ g   h __ __ n

e	o	a

Write the letter of the beginning sounds.

CVC Words

So Many Sounds in a CVC Word

CVC words are simple three-letter words that are made up of a consonant + a vowel + a consonant. If you break a CVC word up into sounds, you will hear three distinct phonemes. Examples of CVC words include cat, sun, pig, dog. the word <u>cat</u> is made up of three sounds — C / A / T — Together these sounds produce the spoken word **cat**. Whereas in segmenting, the word cat is made up of three phonemes — <u>beginning</u>, <u>middle</u> and <u>end</u>.

Write each CVC word in the box below the picture.

cat	dog	sun
bat	bus	pot
bed	web	box
leg	fox	men
pig	gum	wig
lip	pin	log

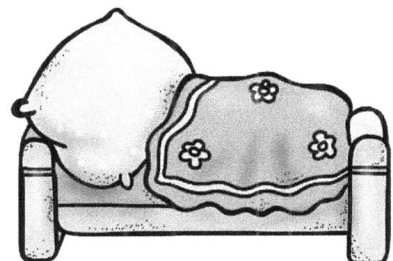

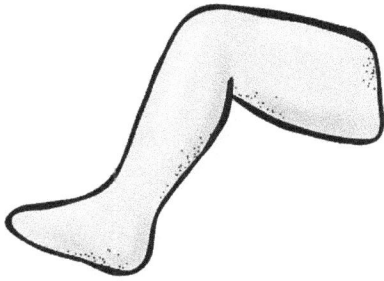

Primer-Kindergarten Sight Word List

Let's now discuss sight words.

Sight words are the words that appear most frequently in our reading and writing, as these are common words that a child recognizes instantly without sounding them. Many sight words are tricky to read and spell as they aren't spelled the way they sound. Therefore, sight words are often very tricky for students to sound out. Recognizing words by sight helps children become fast readers. According to a study, up to 75% of the words used in text written for young readers are sight words.

For example: I, you, he, she, with, this, that, come, some, etc.

The goal is for all Primer Kindergarteners to know 100 sight words by the end of the school year. Once students have learned the alphabet, they can start learning their sight words. Teach 10 new words each month. By the end of the school year, when the students learn these 100 sight words they will be ready for kindergarten and able to read simple stories! Please practice these words with your students every week.

Sight Word List

List 1	List 2	List 3	List 4	List 5
I	like	to	are	do
can	a	have	for	and
we	see	is	you	what
the	go	play	this	little
at	in	come	here	his
am	of	on	she	two
it	us	be	run	love
up	by	big	off	but
no	eat	one	so	all
yes	was	has	want	saw

Sight Word List

List 6	List 7	List 8	List 9	List 10
said	he	my	five	yellow
there	as	me	seven	red
him	look	where	eight	blue
that	with	jump	your	white
got	they	went	because	black
not	three	four	out	brown
too	six	ten	from	green
why	where	get	who	purple
first	day	away	her	pink
new	could	came	then	nine

Sight Word Pratice

Say the word:

a

Circle the sight word:

a	d	l
a	p	a
b	r	a

Trace the word:

a

Write the word:

- - - - - - - - - - - - - - -

Color the letters in the sight word:

a	i	e	d	r
y	s	u	l	n
p	k	h	f	e

Color the word:

a

Complete the sentence:

I can see _____ frog.

Say the word:

and

Trace the word:

and

Write the word:

Color the word:

and

Circle the sight word:

and	end	and
are	ant	and
and	amd	arm

Color the letters in the sight word:

a	i	e	d	r
y	s	u	l	n
p	k	h	f	e

Complete the sentence:

I like cats_____dogs.

Say the word:

go

Trace the word:

go

Write the word:

Color the word:

go

Circle the sight word:

go	to	so
ge	go	og
go	no	go

Color the letters in the sight word:

t	i	e	d	g
y	s	o	l	n
p	k	h	f	e

Complete the sentence:

I can ___ for a run.

Say the word: I

Trace the word: I

Write the word:

- -

_____

Color the word: I

Circle the sight word:

I	a	in
at	I	an
I	go	I

Color the letters in the sight word:

a	i	e	d	r
y	s	u	l	m
p	k	h	f	e

Complete the sentence:

_____ **like to bake.**

Say the word:

is

Trace the word:

is

Write the word:

- -

Color the word:

is

Circle the sight word:

in	is	it
is	if	is
id	is	iz

Color the letters in the sight word:

t	i	e	d	r
y	s	u	l	n
p	k	h	f	e

Complete the sentence:

My hat ___ red.

Say the word:

me

Trace the word:

me

Write the word:

- - - - - - - - - - - - - - - -

_____

Color the word:

me

Circle the sight word:

be	me	my
am	me	he
me	me	mr

Color the letters in the sight word:

o	i	e	m	r
a	k	j	l	n
p	l	o	f	t

Complete the sentence:

She likes ____ .

Say the word:

my

Trace the word:

my

Write the word:

Color the word:

my

Circle the sight word:

me	mo	my
my	ma	my
my	man	me

Color the letters in the sight word:

t	i	e	d	r
y	s	u	l	n
p	k	h	f	m

Complete the sentence:

_____name is Sam.

Say the word:

see

Trace the word:

see

Write the word:

_____

- - - - - - - - - - - - - - -

_____

Color the word:

see

Circle the sight word:

see	bee	sea
see	tee	see
she	see	sew

Color the letters in the sight word:

a	i	e	d	r
y	s	u	l	m
p	k	h	f	e

Complete the sentence:

I _____ a cat.

Say the word:

the

Trace the word:

the

Write the word:

_____

Color the word:

the

Circle the sight word:

ten	tee	the
that	the	this
the	tie	the

Color the letters in the sight word:

t	i	e	d	r
y	s	u	l	n
p	k	h	f	e

Complete the sentence:

_____ **cat is black.**

Say the word:

to

Trace the word:

to

Write the word:

Color the word:

to

Circle the sight word:

no	to	it
to	so	to
on	to	too

Color the letters in the sight word:

t	i	e	d	r
y	s	u	l	n
p	k	h	f	o

Complete the sentence:

Let's walk ____ school.

Numbers

My Brain is Ready to Grow!

0

Count the Dots.

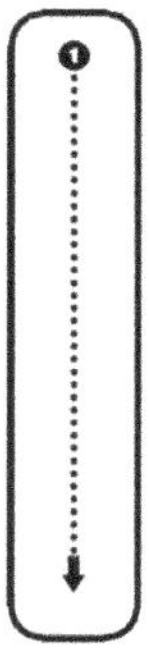

Count the Dots.

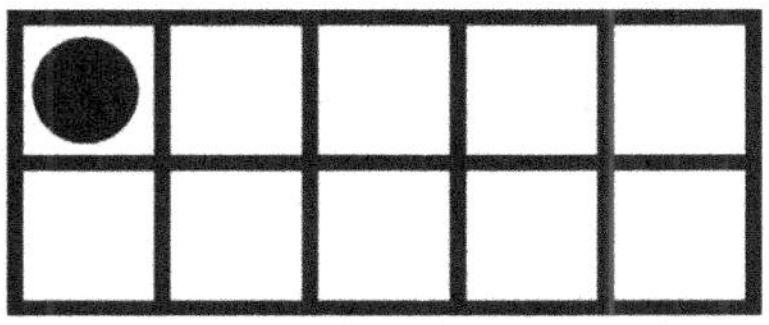

2

Count the Dots.

2 2 2 2
2 2 2 2
2 2 2 2
2 2 2 2
2 2 2 2

2 2 2 2 2 2 2 2
2 2 2 2 2 2 2 2
2 2 2 2 2 2 2 2
2 2 2 2 2 2 2 2

3

Count the Dots.

3 3 3 3

3 3 3 3

3 3 3 3

3 3 3 3

3 3 3 3

3 3 3 3 3 3 3 3 3

3 3 3 3 3 3 3 3 3

3 3 3 3 3 3 3 3 3

3 3 3 3 3 3 3 3 3

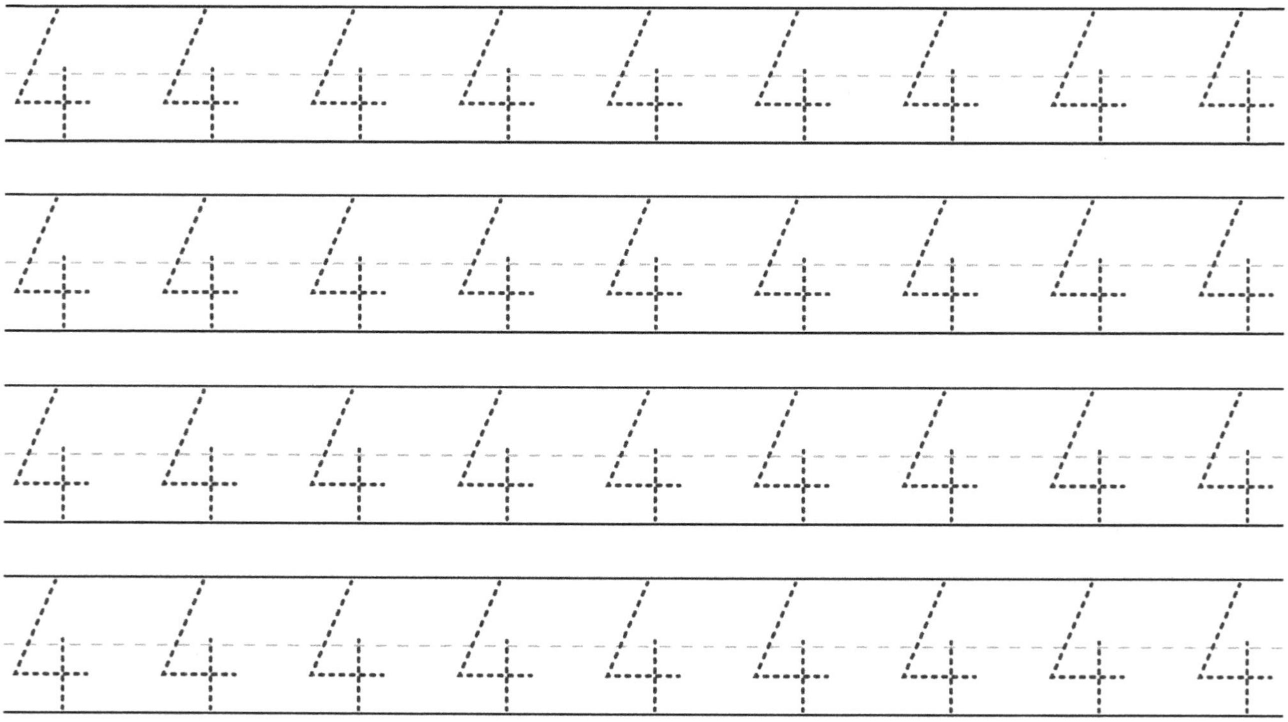

4 4 4 4 4 4 4 4 4

4 4 4 4 4 4 4 4 4

4 4 4 4 4 4 4 4 4

4 4 4 4 4 4 4 4 4

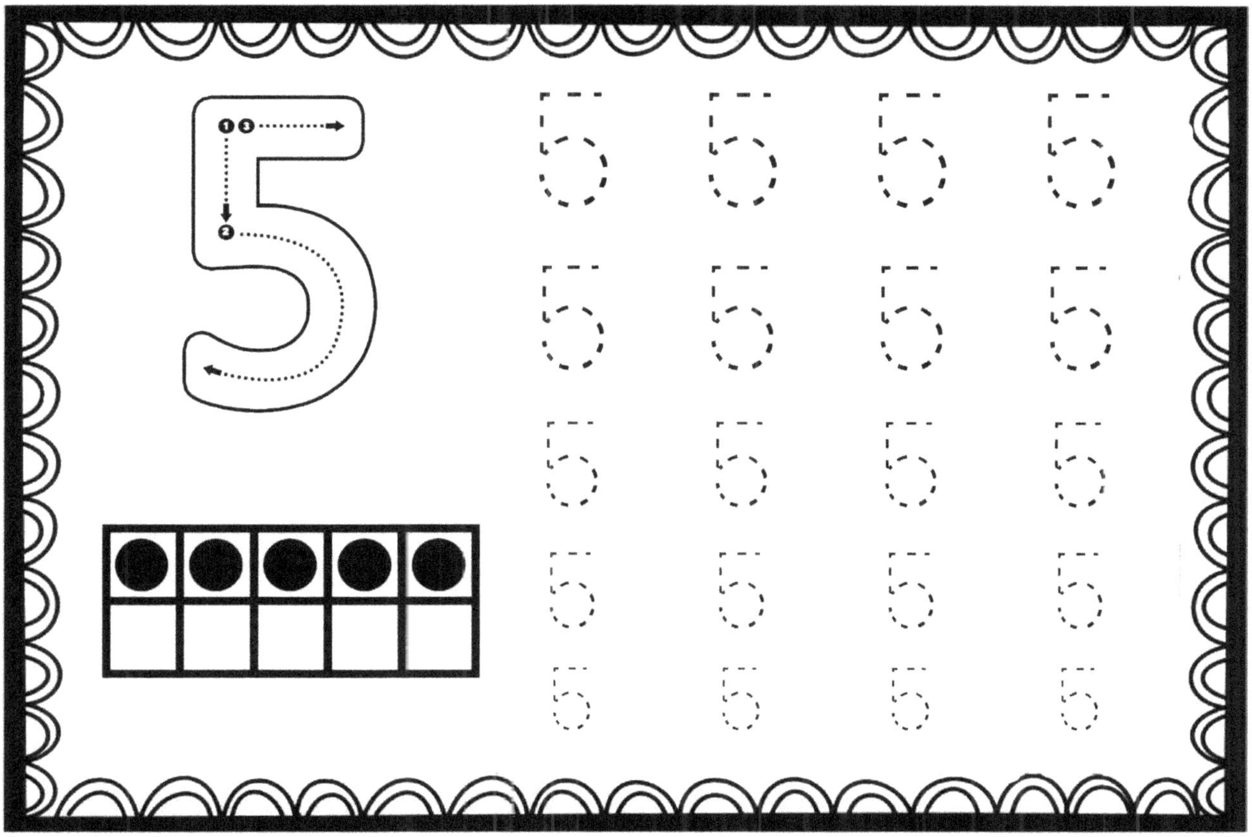
5

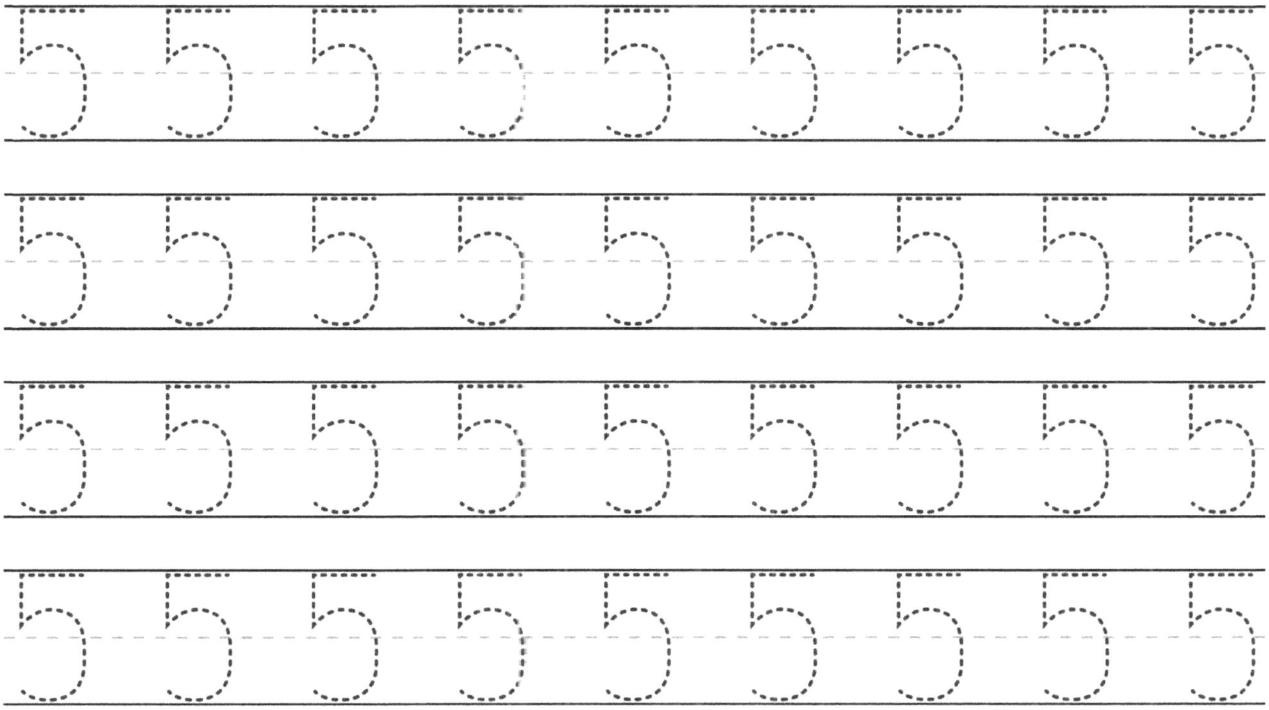

6

Count the Dots.

132

Count the Dots.

133

8

Count the Dots.

134

q

Count the Dots.

q q q q

q q q q

q q q q

q q q q

q q q q

9 9 9 9 9 9 9 9

9 9 9 9 9 9 9 9

9 9 9 9 9 9 9 9

9 9 9 9 9 9 9 9

10

Count the Dots.

10 10 10 10 10 10 10

10 10 10 10 10 10 10

10 10 10 10 10 10 10

10 10 10 10 10 10 10

Tracing Numbers
Trace the numbers to complete the series.

1	1	1	1	1
2	2	2	2	2
3	3	3	3	3
4	4	4	4	4
5	5	5	5	5

Tracing Numbers
Trace the numbers to complete the series.

6   6   6   6   6

7   7   7   7   7

8   8   8   8   8

9   9   9   9   9

10   10   10   10   10

Teen Numbers
Write the teen numbers 11 - 15

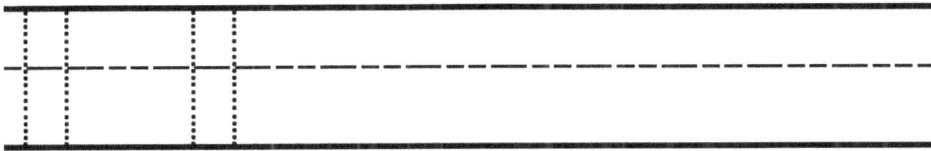

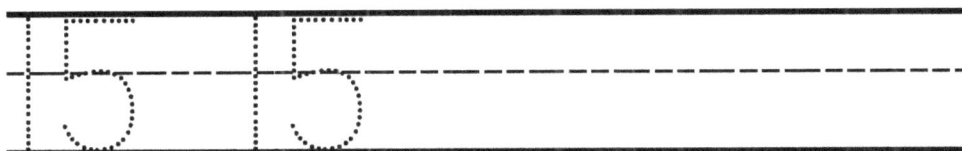

11 _____

12 _____

13 _____

14 _____

15 _____

Teen Numbers
Write the teen numbers 15 - 20

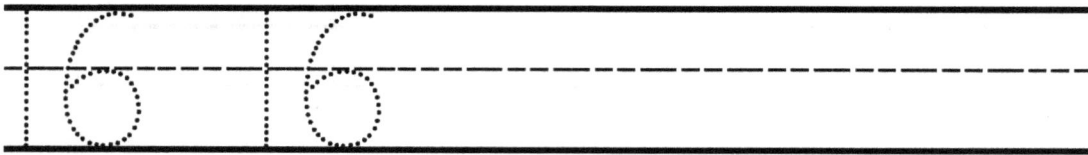

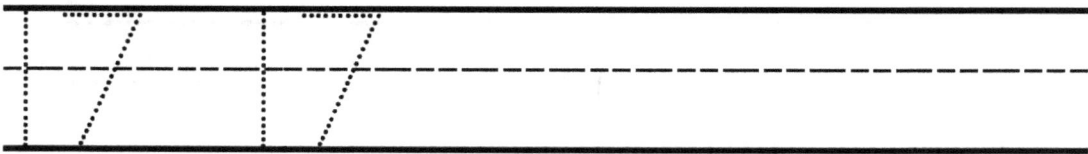

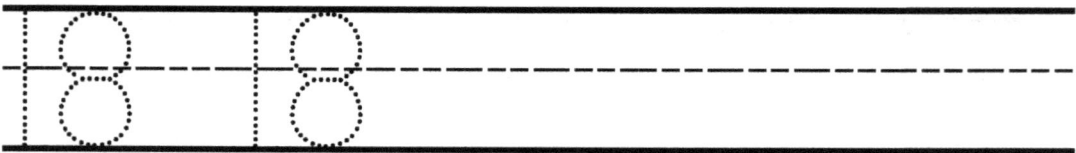

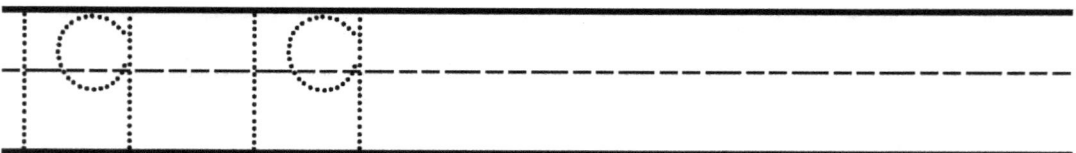

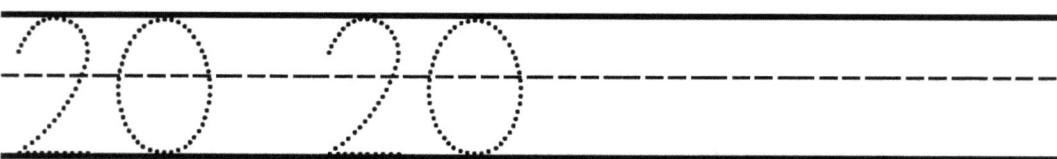

16 16 - - - - - - - - - - - - - -

17 17 - - - - - - - - - - - - - -

18 18 - - - - - - - - - - - - - -

19 19 - - - - - - - - - - - - - -

20 20 - - - - - - - - - - - - - -

Trace the numbers.

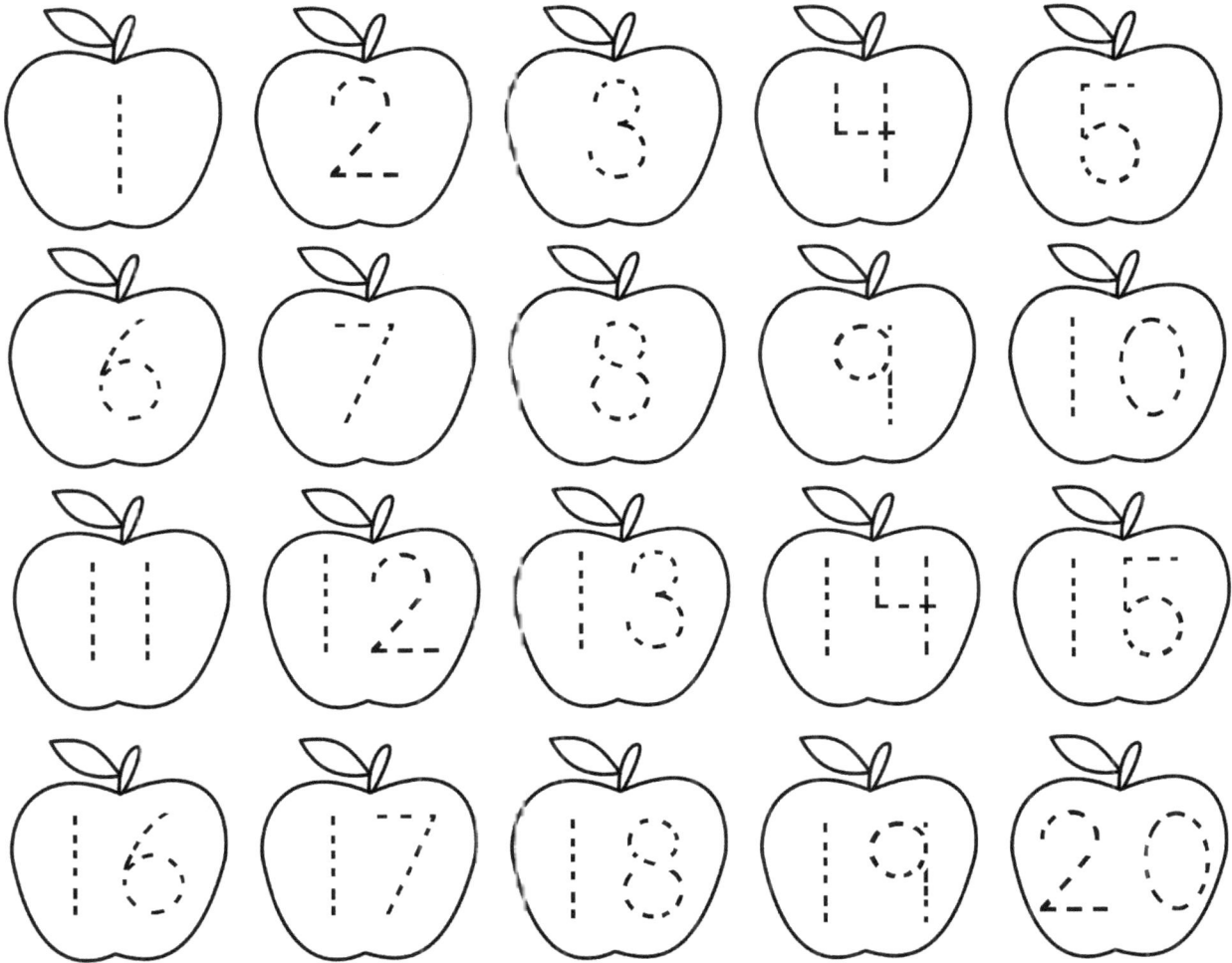

1   2   3   4   5

6   7   8   9   10

11   12   13   14   15

16   17   18   19   20

Writing Numbers Practice
Write each number 2 or 3 times.
Begin at the correct starting point!

0

1

2

3

4

5

6

7

8

9

10

11

12

13

Writing Numbers Practice
Write each number 2 or 3 times.
Begin at the correct starting point!

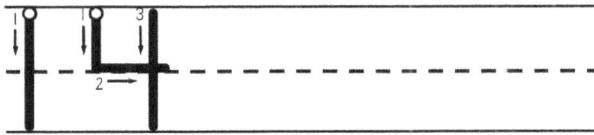

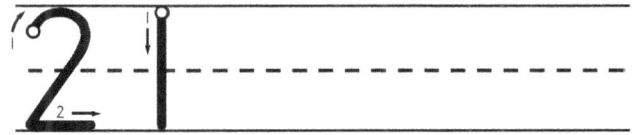

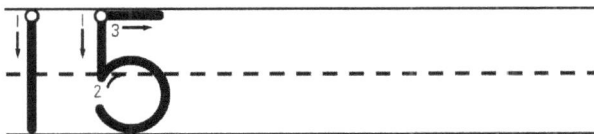

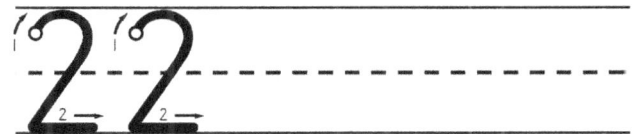

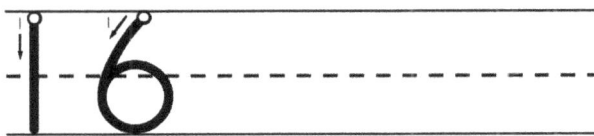

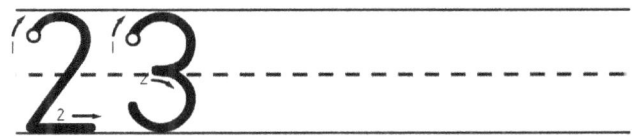

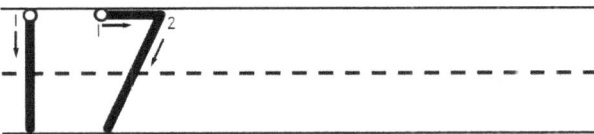

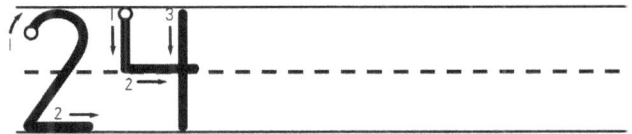

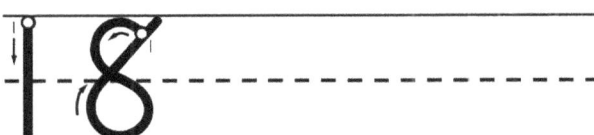

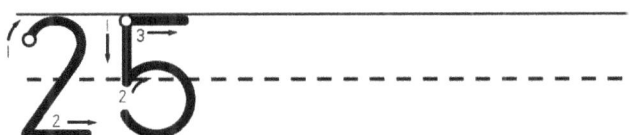

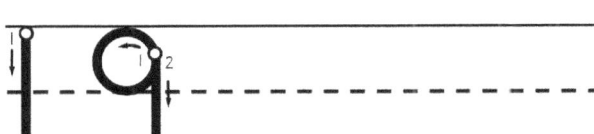

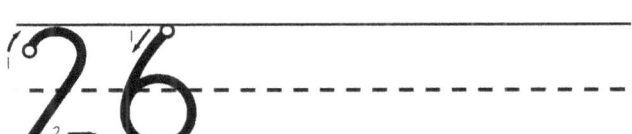

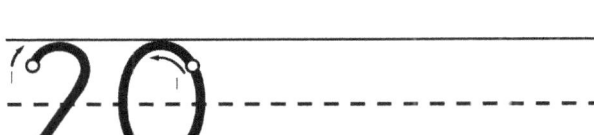

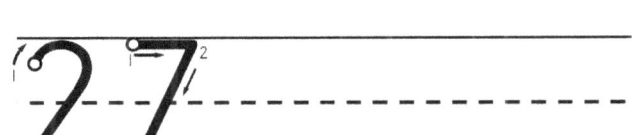

14

21

15

22

16

23

17

24

18

25

19

26

20

27

Writing Numbers Practice
Write each number 2 or 3 times.
Begin at the correct starting point!

28

35

29

36

30

37

31

38

32

39

33

40

34

41

Writing Numbers Practice
Write each number 2 or 3 times.
Begin at the correct starting point!

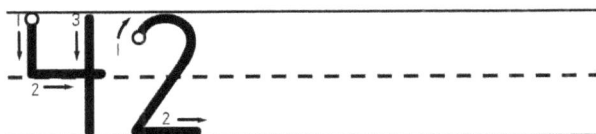

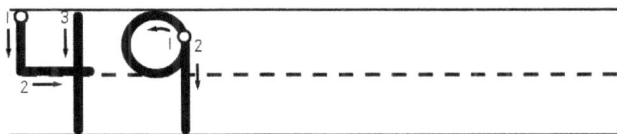

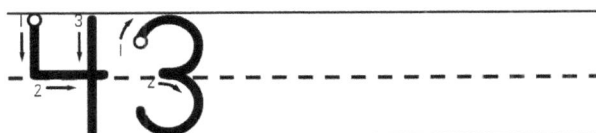

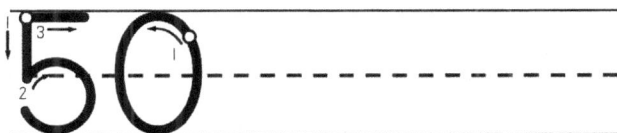

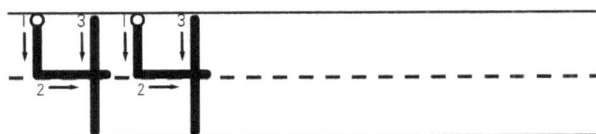

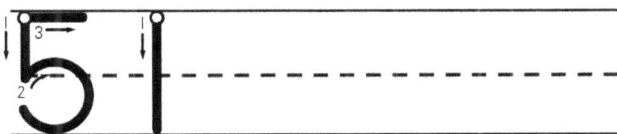

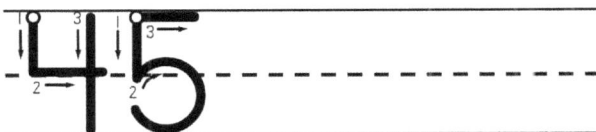

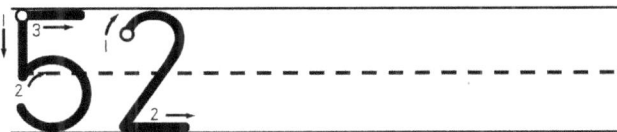

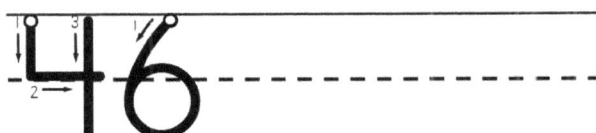

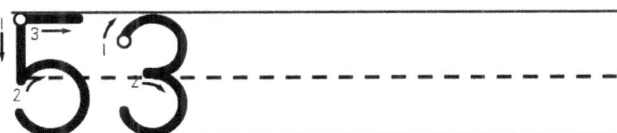

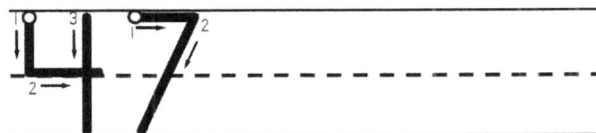

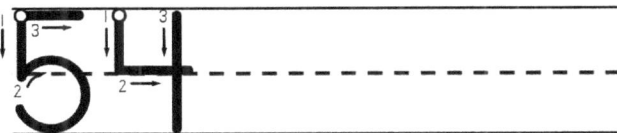

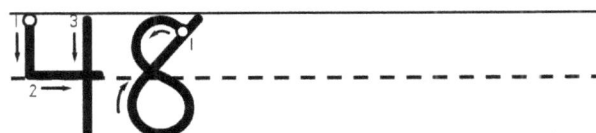

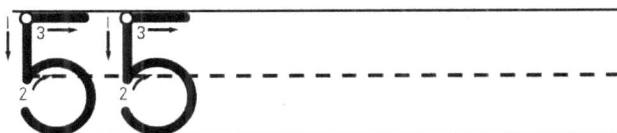

42

43

44

45

46

47

48

49

50

51

52

53

54

55

Writing Numbers Practice
Write each number 2 or 3 times.
Begin at the correct starting point!

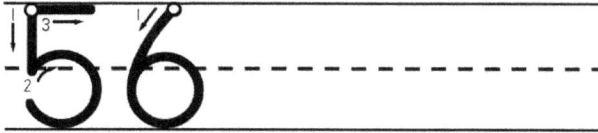

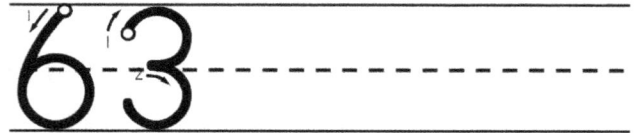

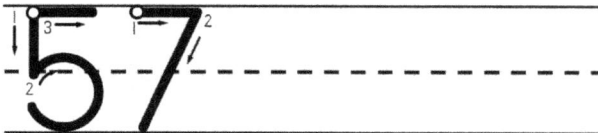

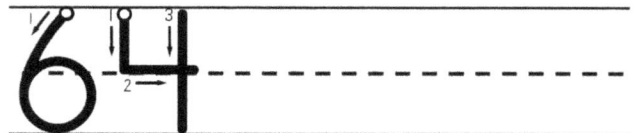

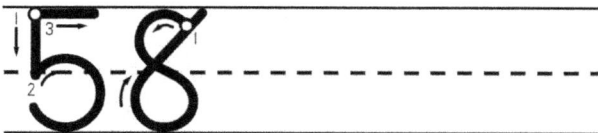

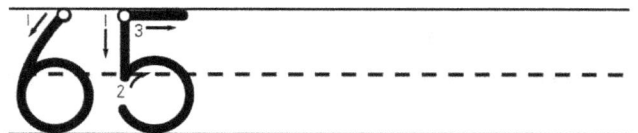

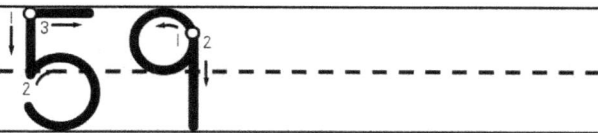

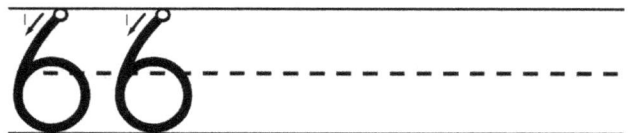

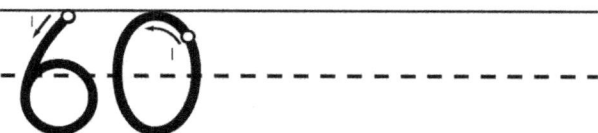

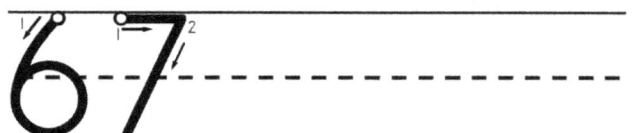

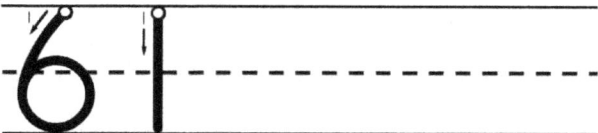

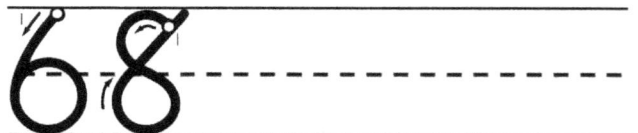

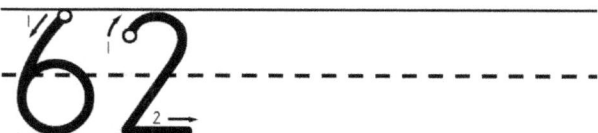

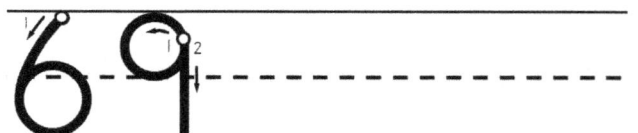

56

57

58

59

60

61

62

63

64

65

66

67

68

69

Writing Numbers Practice
Write each number 2 or 3 times.
Begin at the correct starting point!

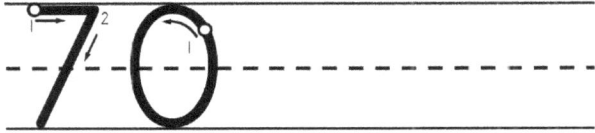

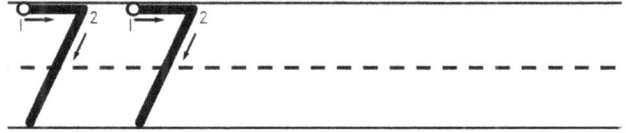

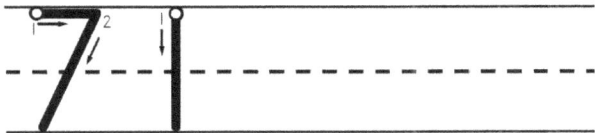

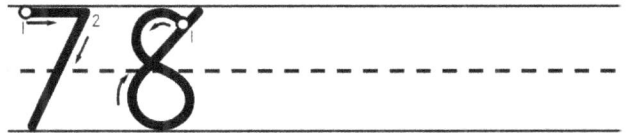

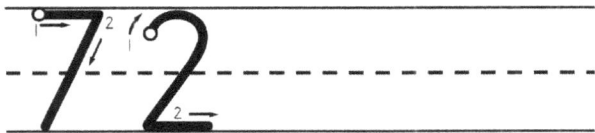

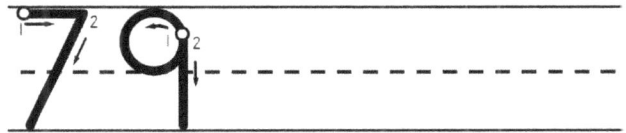

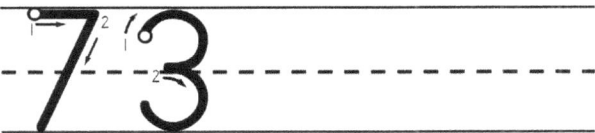

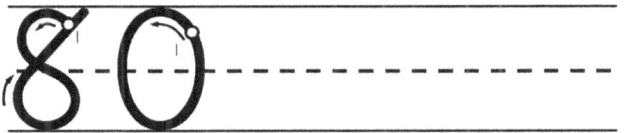

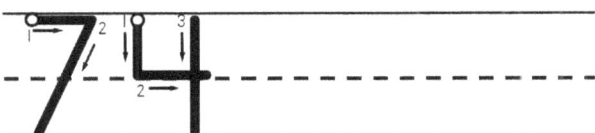

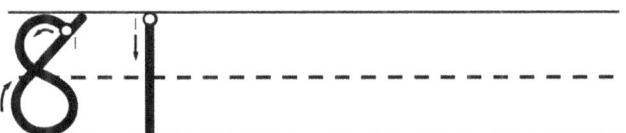

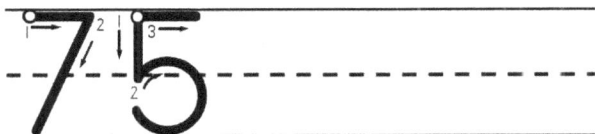

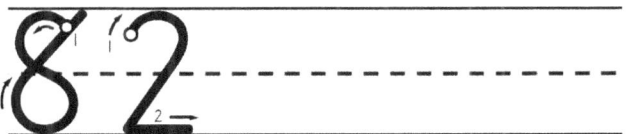

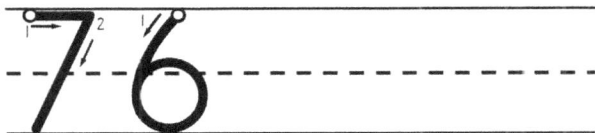

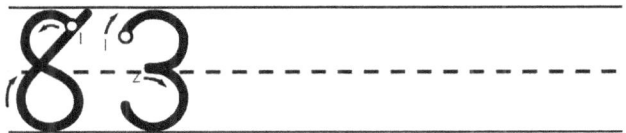

70

77

71

78

72

79

73

80

74

81

75

82

76

83

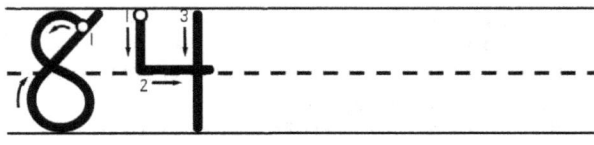

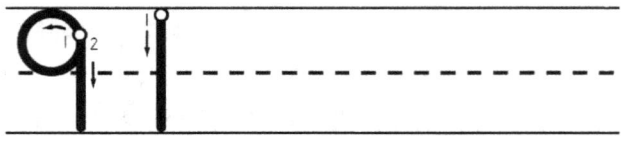

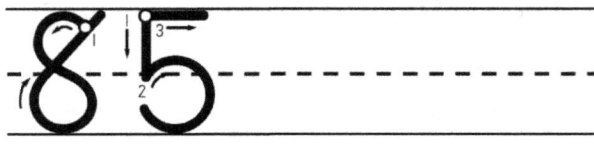

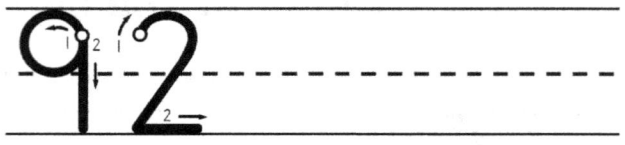

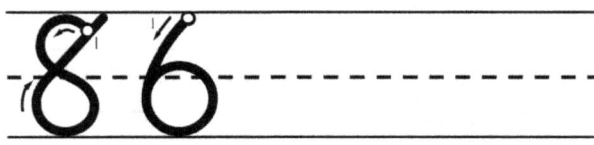

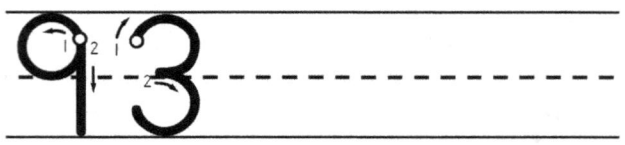

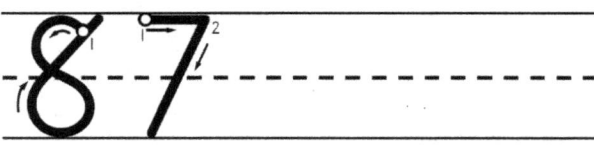

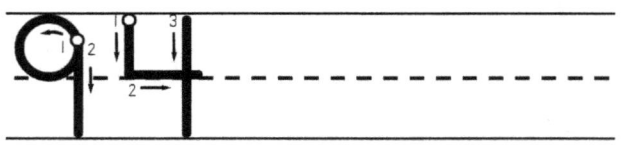

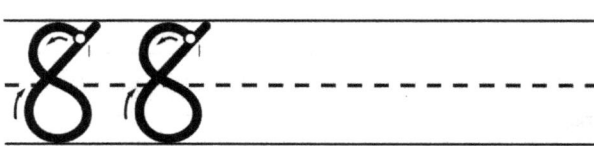

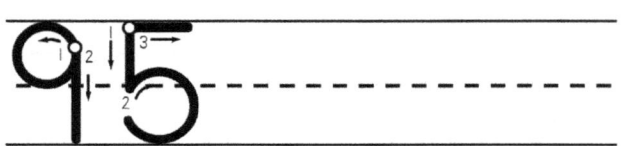

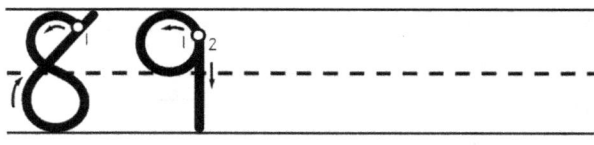

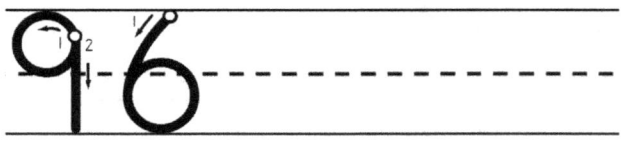

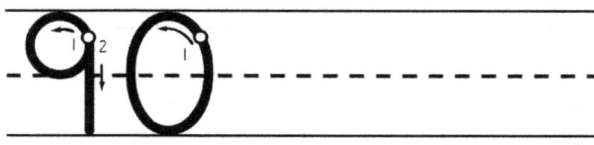

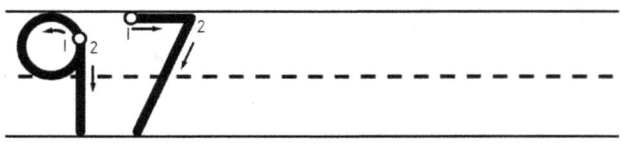

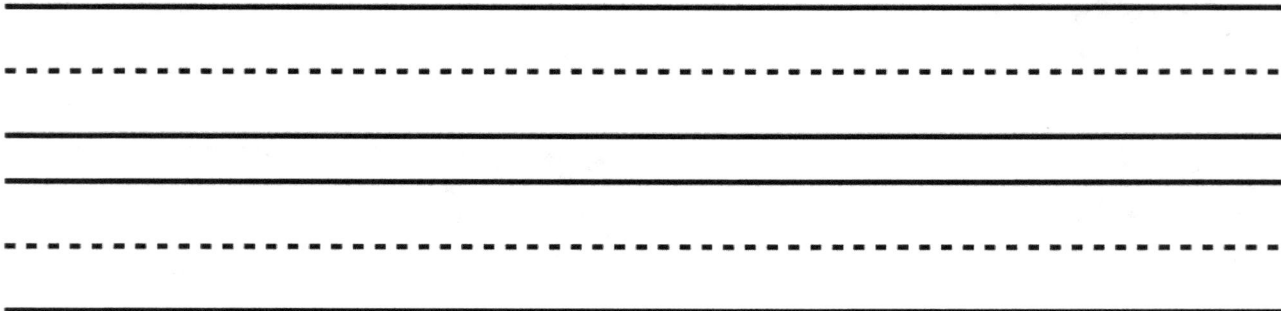

Write each number 1 - 33.
Begin at the correct starting point!

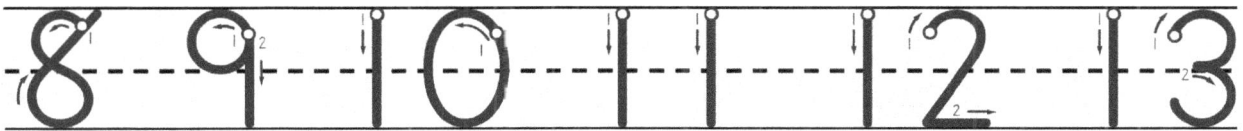

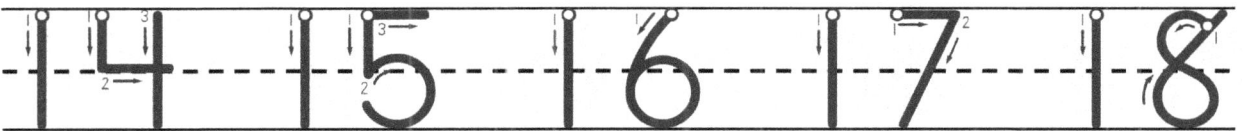

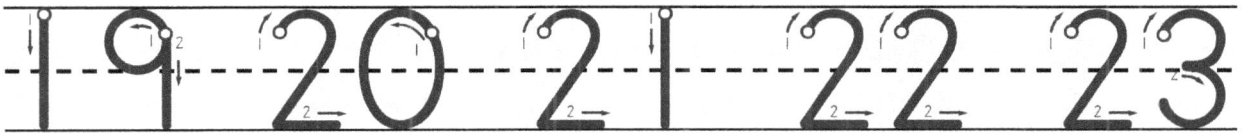

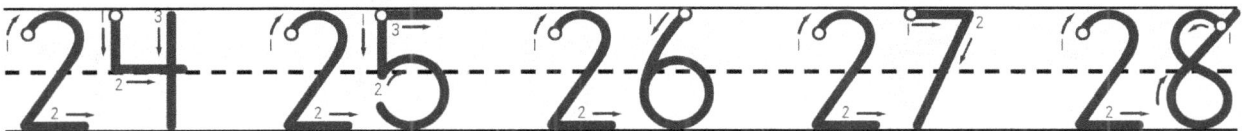

0 1 2 3 4 5 6 7

8 9 10 11 12 13

14 15 16 17 18

19 20 21 22 23

24 25 26 27 28

29 30 31 32 33

Write each number 34 - 63.
Begin at the correct starting point!

34   35   36   37   38

39   40   41   42   43

44   45   46   47   48

49   50   51   52   53

54   55   56   57   58

59   60   61   62   63

64 65 66 67 68

69 70 71 72 73

74 75 76 77 78

79 80 81 82 83

84 85 86 87 88

89 90 91 92 93

94 95 96 97 98

99 100

Numbers 1-50
Fill in the Missing Numbers

1		3	4	
	7	8		10
11	12		14	15
16			19	
	22	23		25
26		28		30
31	32			35
36		38	39	
	42			45
46		48		50

Numbers 51-100
Fill in the Missing Numbers

51		53		55
56	57		59	
		63		65
	67		69	
71	72			75
		78	79	
81		83		85
86		88		
	92		94	95
96		98		100

Numbers 1-50
Fill in the Missing Numbers

1				
				50

Numbers 51-100
Fill in the Missing Numbers

51				
				100

Learn your number words
1 - 10

1		one
2		two
3		three
4		four
5		five
6		six
7		seven
8		eight
9		nine
10		ten

Write Your Number Word

0

zero

Write Your Number Word

I

one

Write Your Number Word

2

two

Write Your Number Word

3

three

Write Your Number Word

4

four

161

Write Your Number Word

5

five

Write Your Number Word

6

six

_____

- -

_____

- -

_____

Write Your Number Word

7

seven

Write Your Number Word

8

eight

Write Your Number Word

q

nine

Write Your Number Word

10

ten

Write Your Number Word

11

eleven

_____

- -

_____

- -

_____

Write Your Number Word

12

twelve

Color by Number

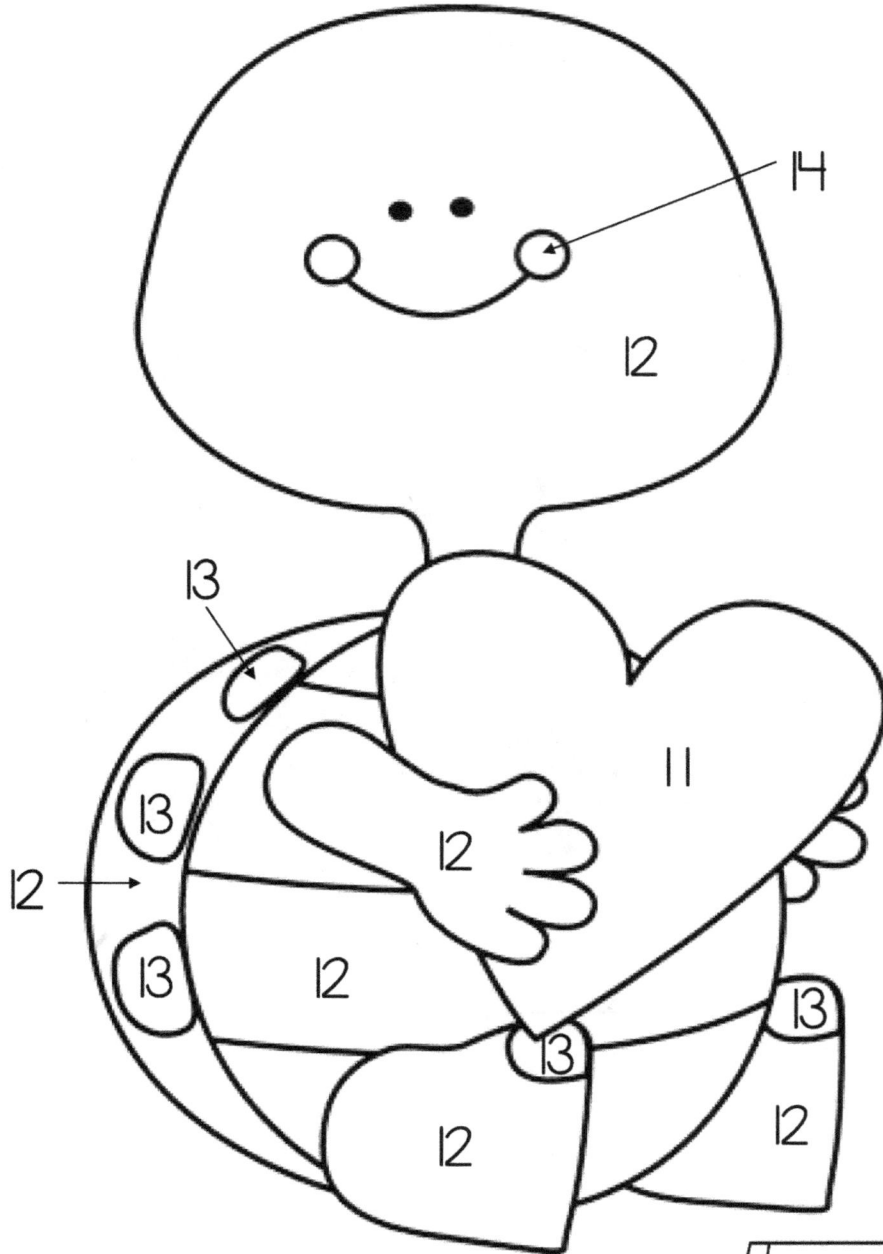

11 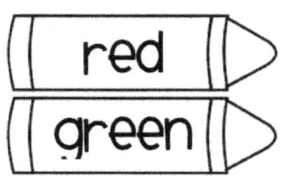 red	13  yellow
12 green	14 pink

Color by Number

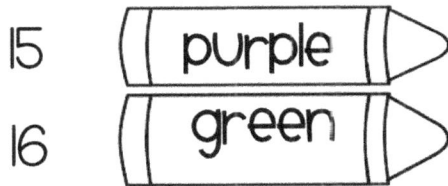

15	purple	17	red
16	green	18	blue

Color by Number Word

0-green

1-blue

2-red

3 - yellow

4 - white

5-purple

6-orange

7 - brown

8 - black

9 - pink

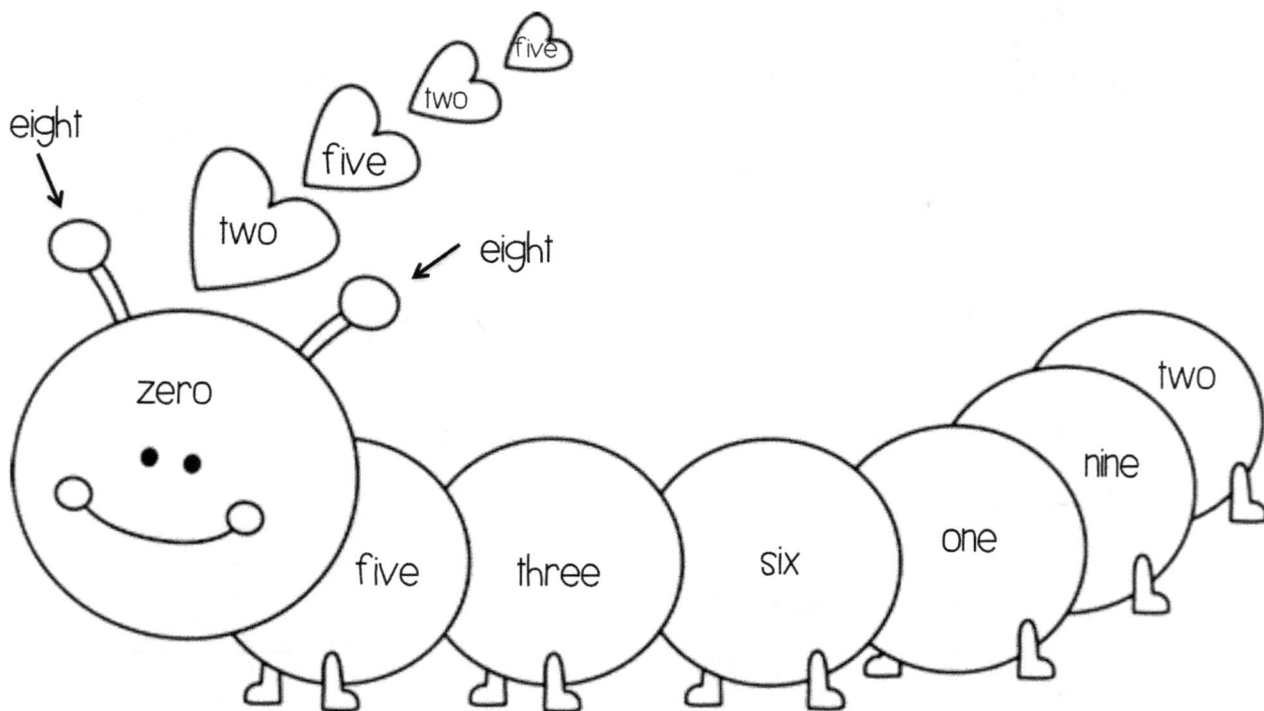

Color and Count — Numbers 1-5
Under the Sea

How many?

Color and Count — Numbers 5-10
Under the Sea

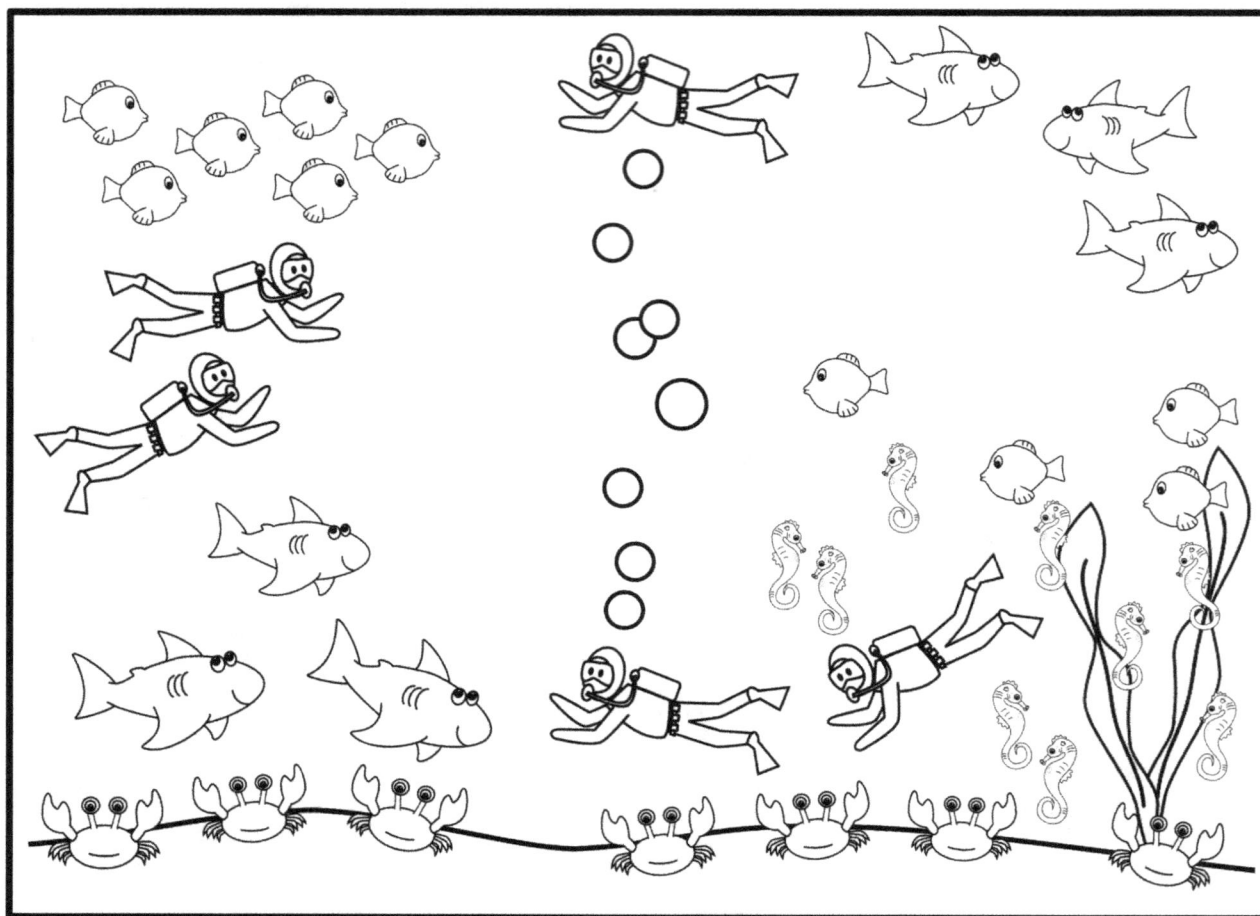

How many?

Shapes and Colors
SHAPES

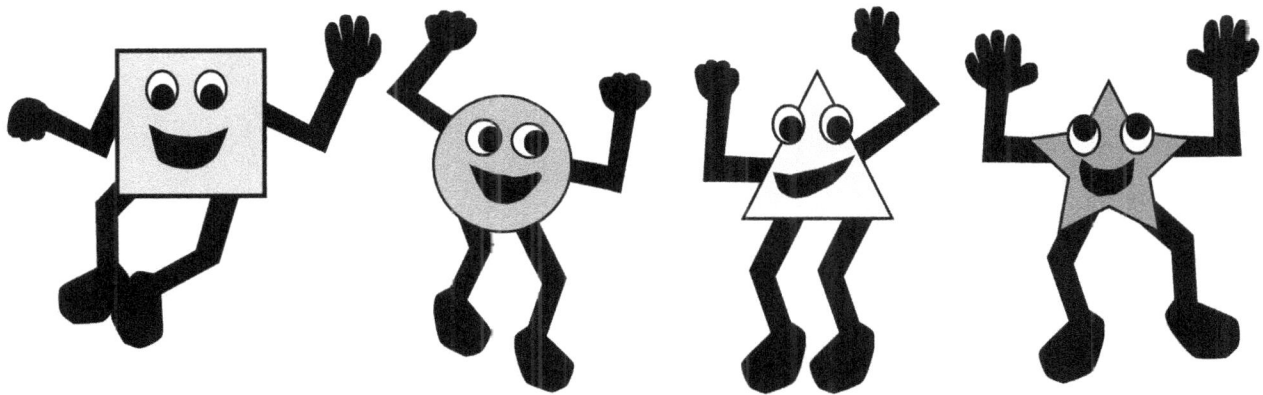

The three basic shapes are a square, a triangle and a circle. The four easiest shapes to learn are circle, square, triangle, and star.

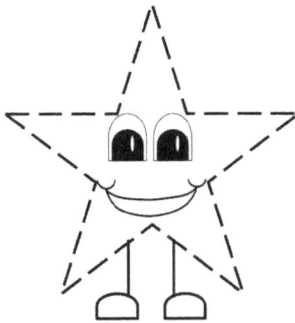

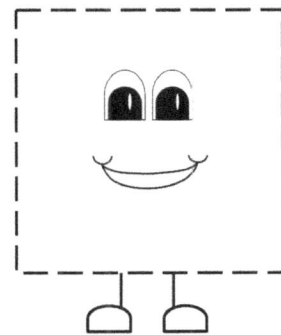

Practice tracing the shapes and their names.
Then color them all in.

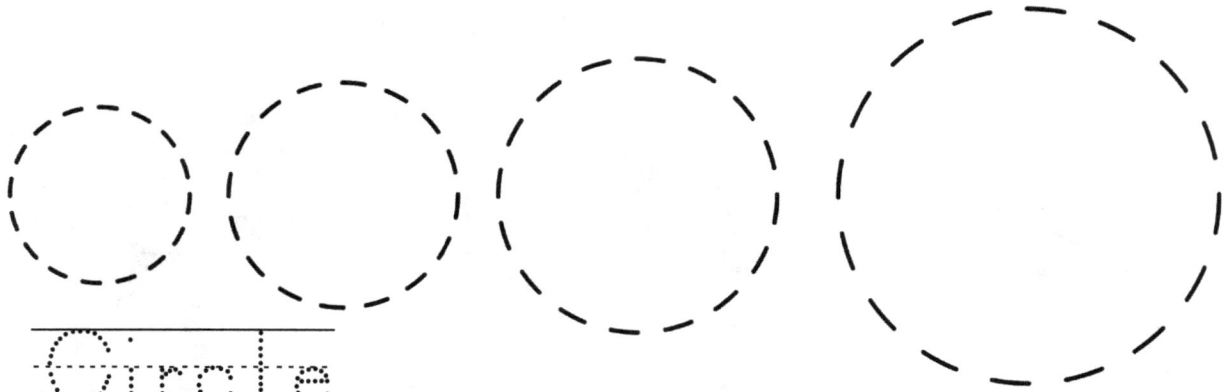

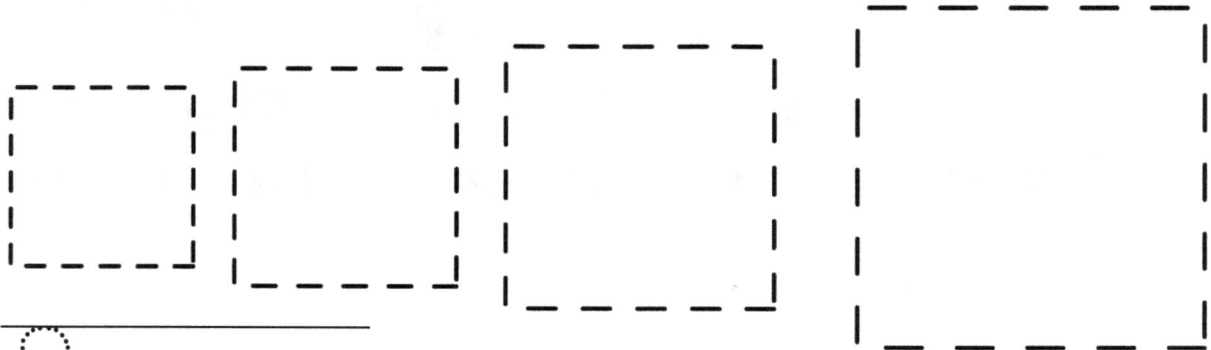

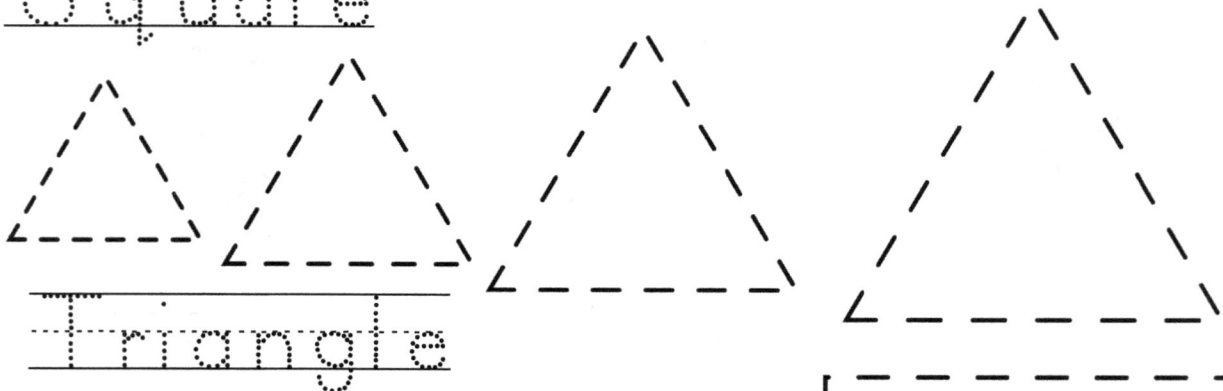

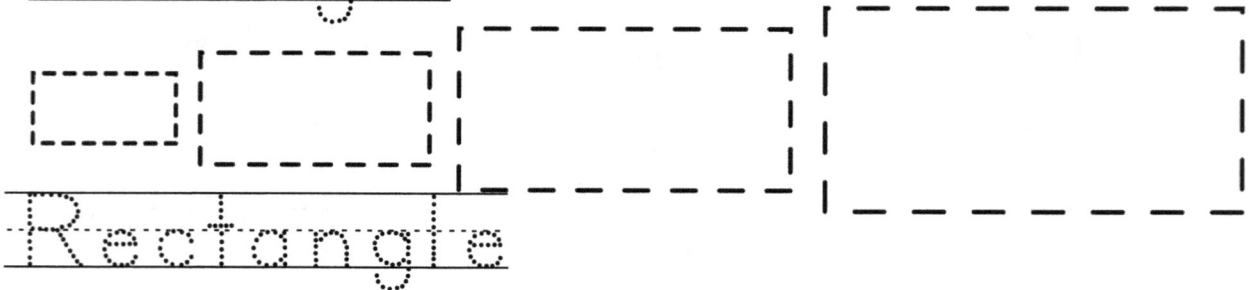

Circle

Square

Triangle

Rectangle

Practice tracing the shapes. Then color them all in.

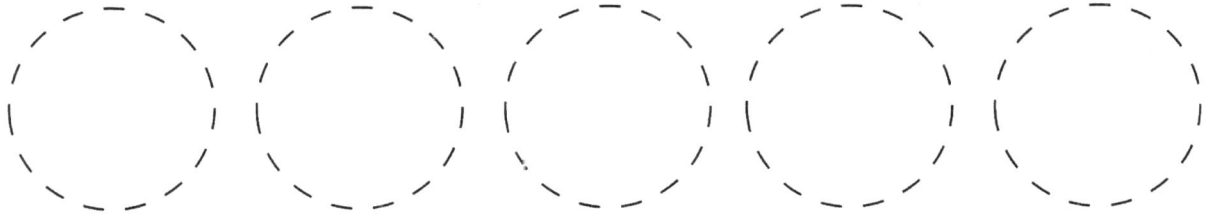

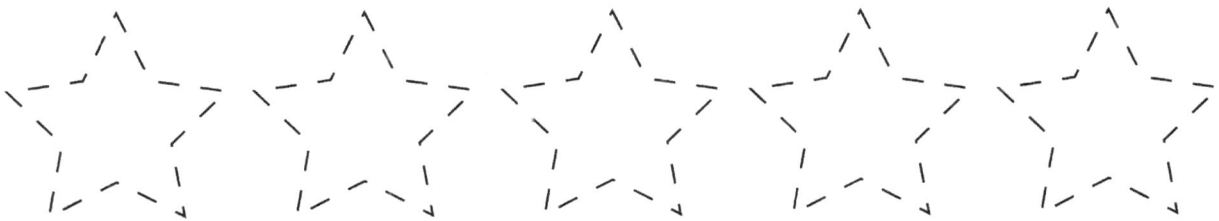

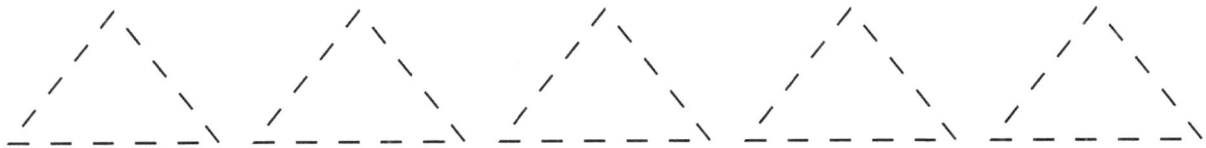

Shape the maze: follow and color the △ 's to find the path to the hole in the ice.

Shape the maze: follow and color the ◯ **'s to help the bear get back to his cave.**

Shape It Up!
Can you write each shape with its name?

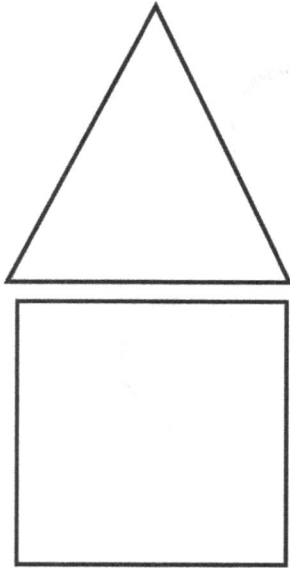

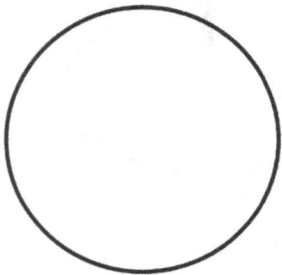

Square
Heart
Star
Circle
Triangle

_____

- - - - - - - - - - - - - - -

_____

_____

- - - - - - - - - - - - - - -

_____

_____

- - - - - - - - - - - - - - -

_____

_____

- - - - - - - - - - - - - - -

_____

_____

- - - - - - - - - - - - - - -

_____

Color Words
My Brain is Ready to Grow!

Name:

I Know My Colors

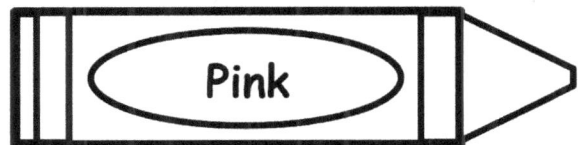

Blue

Red

Yellow

Green

Orange

Purple

White

Brown

Black

Pink

What is red?
Complete each color word:

These things are red.

strawberry

tomato

red

___ ed

___ d

ladybug

apple

Name:

Color 5 things that are red.

What is yellow?
Complete each color word:

These things are yellow.

yellow

banana

___ellow

corn

___llow

lemon

___low

sun

___ow

___w

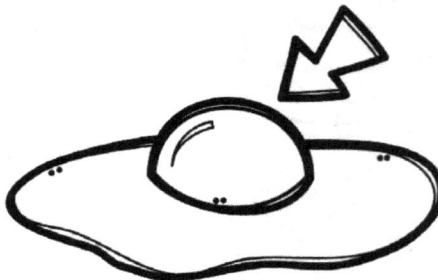
egg yoke

Name: ....

Color 5 things that are yellow.

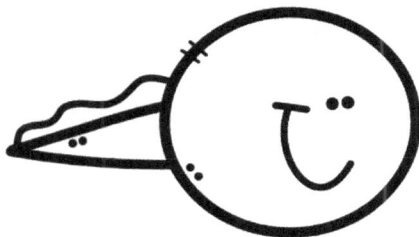

What is green?
Complete each color word:

These things are green.

alligator

green

___reen

___een

turtle

___en

___n

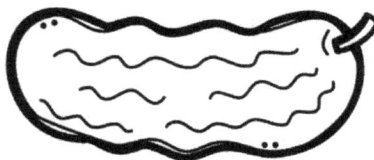

pickle

cactus

frog

Name:

Color 5 things that are green.

What is blue?
Complete each color word:

These things are blue.

blueberries

blue

___lue

bluejay

___ue

blue jeans

___

___e

handicap sign

sky

___

Name:

Color 5 things that are blue.

What is white?
Complete each color word:

These things are white.

white

cloud

___hite

sheep

___ite

___te

ghost

___e

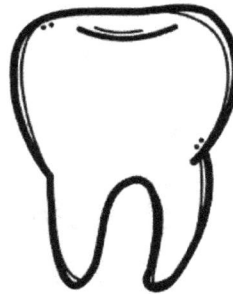
tooth

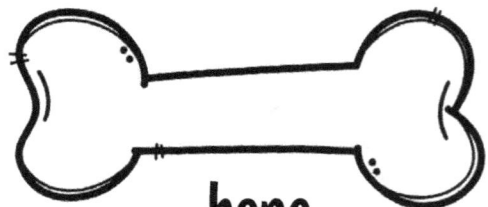
bone

190

Name:

Color 5 things that are white.

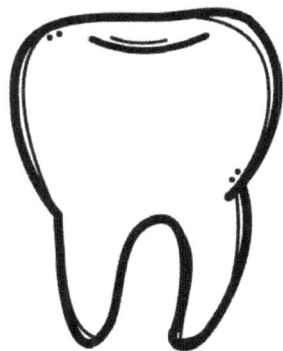

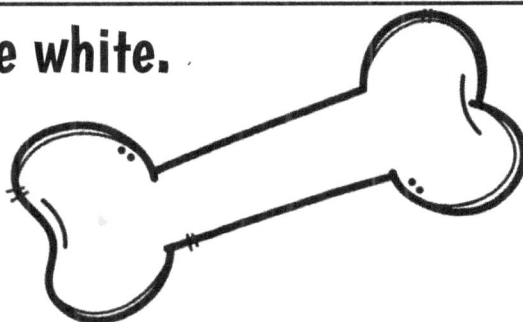

What is orange?
Complete each color word:

These things are orange.

orange

orange

_____range

carrot

_____ange

pumpkin

_____nge

_____ge

basketball

_____e

goldfish

Name: ....

Color 5 things that are orange.

What is brown?
Complete each color word:

brown

___ ___

___rown

___own

___wn

___n

These things are brown.

squirrel

bear

log

acorn
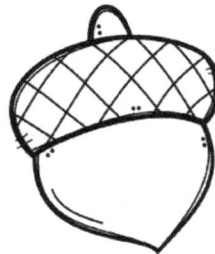

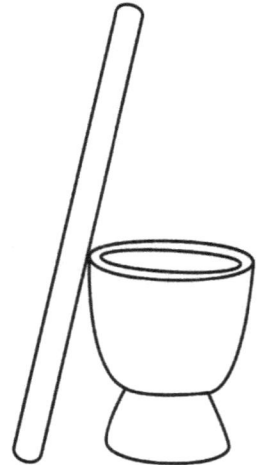
mortar & pestle

194

Name:

Color 5 things that are brown.

What is gray?
Complete each color word:

gray

___**ray**

___**ay**

___**y**

_____

These things are gray.

shark

whistle

coin

elephant

whale

Name:

Color 5 things that are gray.

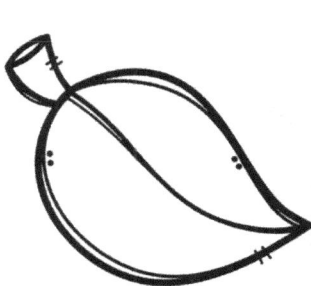

What is purple?
Complete each color word:

These things are purple.

grape jam

purple

_____ urple

_____ rple

African violet

plum

_____ ple

_____ le

eggplant

_____ e

grapes

Color 5 things that are purple.

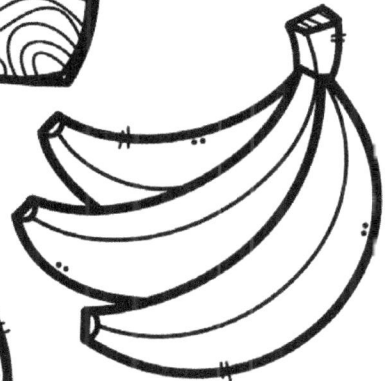

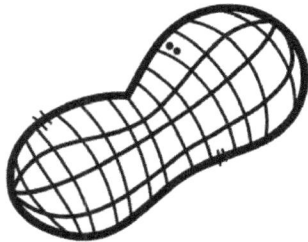

What is pink?
Complete each color word:

These things are pink.

pink

____ink

____nk

____k

____

bubblegum

pig

flamingoes

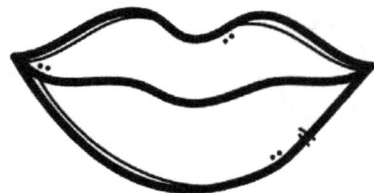

lips

Name: ....

Color 5 things that are pink.

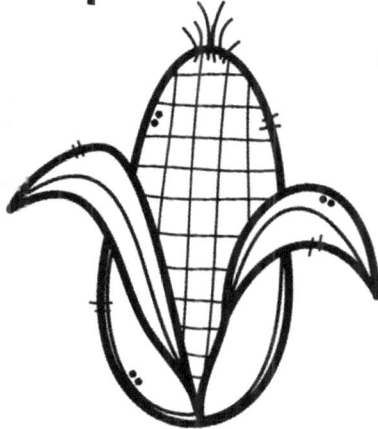

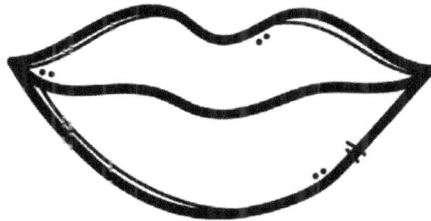

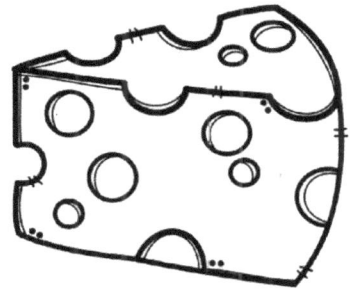

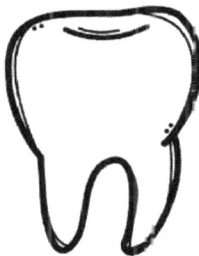

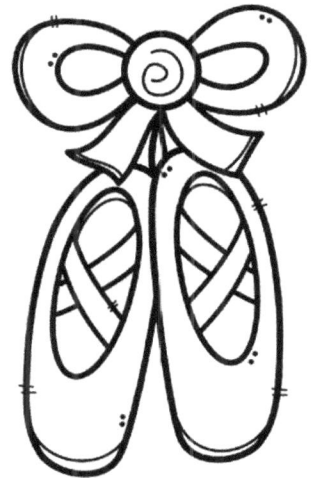

What is black?
Complete each color word:

These things are black.

bat

black

_lack

_ack

_ck

_k

penguin

hat

skunk

spider

Name:

Color 5 things that are black.

Name:

Use the color code to color the picture.

1- red   5- black

2- green   6-yellow

3- pink   7- brown

4- blue

Mixing Some Colors

Now that we have learn our colors, let's try mixing some secondary colors by mixing the primary colors together!

1 - Blue
2 - Yellow
3 - Red
4 - Green
5 - Orange
6 - Purple

What happens when you mix all three of the primary colors?

7- Mystery color!

PRIMARY + PRIMARY = SECONDARY

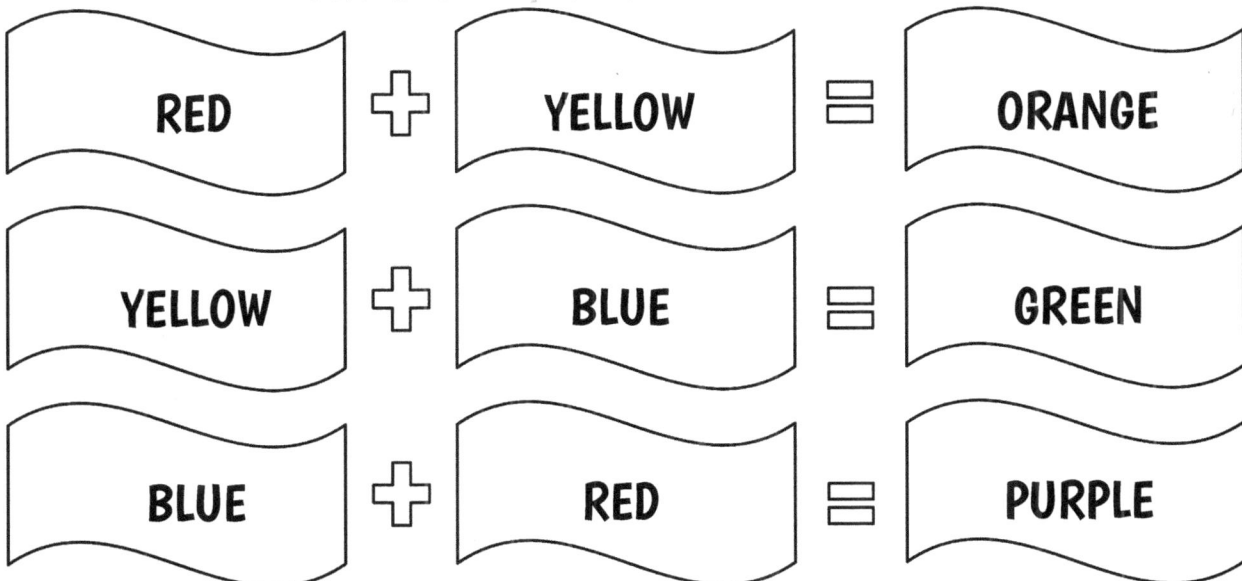

RED	+	YELLOW	=	ORANGE
YELLOW	+	BLUE	=	GREEN
BLUE	+	RED	=	PURPLE

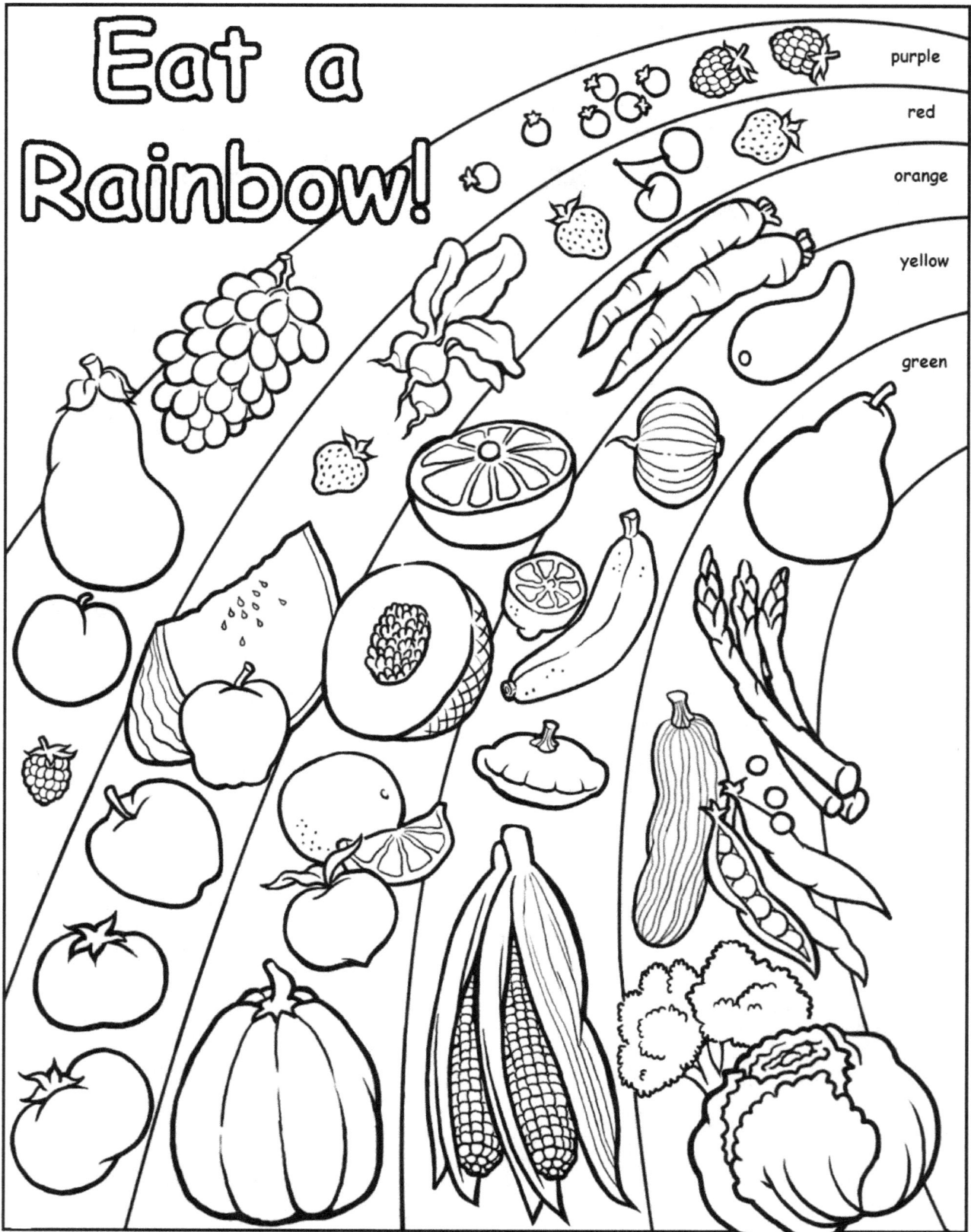

Eat a Rainbow!

purple

red

orange

yellow

green

Good Character Building

Good Behavior / Bad Behavior

Behavior means the way in which a person acts. We all act in a particular way by what we choose to do. It is good to think carefully before you decide what to do. That way, you select the Good Choice and not the Bad Choice.

Honesty

Honesty means telling the truth. Telling the truth can be hard, especially when you've done something wrong. But when you tell the truth, you show people you respect and care about them. When you tell a lie, it makes your mistakes even bigger. The opposite of honesty is dishonesty. Dishonesty makes people feel bad. It makes you feel bad too. When you are honest, you can make your mistakes better.

Good Choice = Positive Behavior

- Listening to the teacher.
- Focusing on my work.
- Staying on task.
- Staying in my seat.
- Raising my hand.
- Working together.
- Giving a high-five.
- Cleaning up.
- Helping a friend.
- Being a good friend.
- Not giving up.
- If at first you don't succeed, try. . . try. . . try again.
- Being appreciative.
- Listening and thinking.
- Staying quiet in line.
- Being responsible.
- Using self-control.

Bad Choice = Negative Behavior

- Not working as a team.
- Not telling the truth.
- Not listening.
- Pushing & throwing things.
- Using unkind words.
- Drawing/scribbling on someone's paper.
- Copying someone else's work.
- Making a mess.
- Ripping paper.
- Distracting others.
- Invading personal space.
- Kicking objects or kicking someone.
- Teasing.
- Pushing someone.
- Stealing from someone.

Being Independent

Working independently means you can do it by yourself. It is important for you to do things independently. This means you complete them by yourself. The teacher is here if you need him/her, but you should also try to figure it out by yourself first. It will make you feel *good* about yourself when you can complete it on your own.

Responsible for Items — take care of your school supplies, don't be wasteful with your supplies and other things. Situations of being wasteful could be taking more food at lunch than you will eat, throwing away paper that could still be used, or throwing away a glue stick that is not empty yet. Some examples of not being wasteful could be saving half a sandwich for later or using the back of a paper to draw a picture. Clean up after yourself and help others. Be more responsible for your items by keeping track of them and knowing where you put them.

Being a Leader and not a follower — it is better to be a leader and lead people to do the right thing, than to be a follower following someone who is doing the wrong thing; doing the right thing for NO reward, and thinking of others before yourself.

Good Manners Alphabet

A great citizen has good manners, from A to Z.

	I can learn my good manner alphabets.
A	Arrive On Time.
B	Be patient.
C	Close Doors Quietly.
D	Don't Pout.
E	Elbows Off Table.
F	Finders Are Not Keepers.
G	Go To Bed Without Fussing.
H	Hand Stuff Over.
I	Interrupting Is Not Nice.
J	Jokes Should Not Hurt Others.
K	Knock And Wait to hear, "Come In."
L	Listen Closely.
M	"May I?" Is A Good Way To Ask.
N	No Hats At The Table, Please.
O	Obey Rules.
P	Pay Attention to details.

I can learn my good manner alphabets.

Q	Quit Wanting To Be First.
R	Role-model Kindness To Others.
S	Share Your Toys.
T	"Thank You" and "Please" Are Good Courtesies.
U	Use Positive Words.
V	Views of Others Must Be Handled Tenderly.
W	Wait Your Turn.
X	"eXcuse me, please," is a key phrase.
Y	"Yes" sounds better than "yep" or "yeah."
Z	Zoom! Zoom! is for outdoors!

Introducing Oneself

Review how the student is to introduce themselves to someone new. Have them repeat the phrase, "Hello, my name is _____."

52 Bible Verses to Memorize

Acts 16:31 Believe in the Lord Jesus Christ, and you will be saved.	**1 John 4:19** We love because he first loved us.	**Proverbs 14:5** A honest witness does not lie, a false witness breathes lies.
James 1:17 Every good gift and every perfect gift is from above.	**Psalm 145:9** The LORD is good to all.	**Genesis 16:13** You are the God who sees.
Matthew 22:39 You shall love your neighbor as yourself.	**Numbers 6:24** The Lord bless you and keep you.	**Colossians 3:2** Set your minds on things above, not on earthly things.
Philippians 4:4 Rejoice in the Lord always. I will say it again: Rejoice!	**Colossians 3:16** Let the word of Christ dwell in you richly.	**1 John 5:3** This is love for God: to obey his commands.
Ephesians 4:30 And do not grieve the Holy Spirit.	**Proverbs 3:5** Trust in the Lord with all your heart.	**Hebrews 13:8** Jesus Christ is the same yesterday, today and forever.
Romans 10:13 Everyone who calls on the name of the Lord will be saved.	**Romans 3:23** All people have sinned and come short of the glory of God.	**Matthew 5:14** You are the light of the world.
Psalm 150:6 Let everything that has breath praise the Lord.	**Psalm 145:9** The Lord is good to all.	**Colossians 3:20** Children, obey your parents in all things.
Matthew 28:20 I am with you always.	**1 John 3:23** Love one another.	**Psalm 56:3** "When I am afraid, I put my trust in You.

Ephesians 4:32 Be kind to one another.	**Psalm 119:105** Your word is a lamp to my feet and a light for my path.	**Psalm 118:24** This is the day the Lord has made; Let us rejoice and be glad in it.
Psalm 136:1 Give thanks to the Lord, for he is good. His love endures forever.	**Luke 6:31** Do to others as you would have them do to you.	**Philippians 4:13** "I can do all things through Christ who gives me strength."
Psalm 138:1 I will praise thee with my whole heart.	**John 10:11** I am the good shepherd.	**Matthew 6:24** No one can serve two masters.
Proverbs 30:5 Every word of God proves true.	**Ephesians 6:1** Children, obey your parents in the Lord, for this is right.	**John 11:35** Jesus wept.
Deuteronomy 6:5 You shall love the LORD your God with all your heart and with all your soul and with all your might.	**Corinthians 10:31** Whatever you do, do everything for the glory of God.	**Psalm 19:1** The heavens declare the glory of God.
Ecclesiastes 12:13 Fear God and keep his commandments.	**Matthew 28:6** He is not here, he is risen!	**Acts 5:29** We must obey God rather than men.
1 Thessalonians 5:17 Pray without ceasing.	**Isaiah 26:4** Trust in the Lord forever, for the Lord God is an everlasting rock.	**Psalm 46:10** Be still, and know that I am God.

Proverbs 2:6 The Lord gives wisdom.	Psalm 1:6 The LORD knows the way of the righteous, but the way of the wicked will perish.	Psalm 150:6 Let everything that has breath praise the LORD!
Galatians 6:7 Do not be deceived: God is not mocked, for whatever one sows, that will he also reap.		

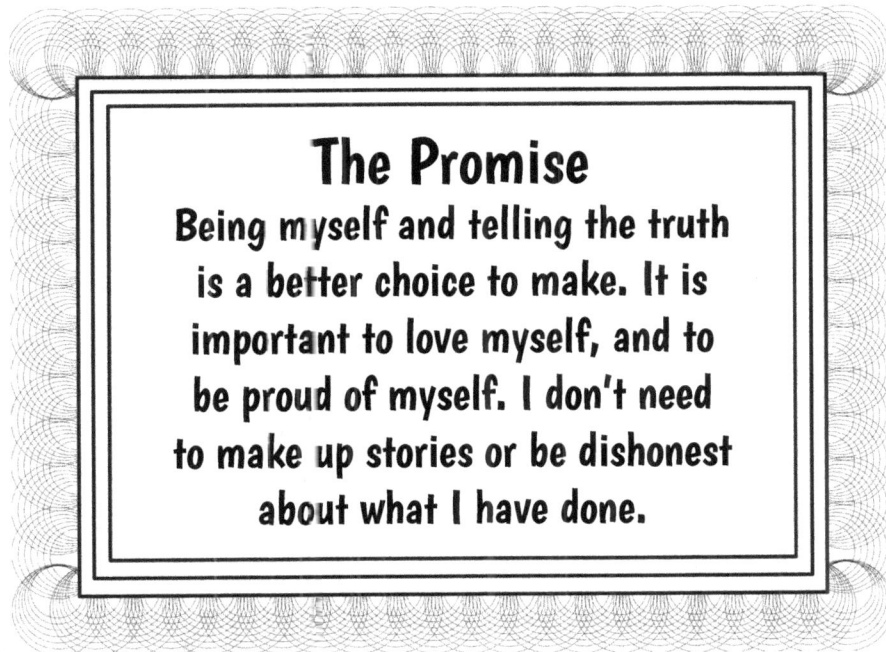

The Promise
Being myself and telling the truth is a better choice to make. It is important to love myself, and to be proud of myself. I don't need to make up stories or be dishonest about what I have done.

Friendship

Friendship is a warm and kind feeling or attatude toward someone.
You can be a friend.
I am a good friend when I . . .

- Give and share.
- Help.
- Show love.
- Care.
- Tell the truth.
- Listen.

Lend a Hand

YOU DID IT!

Name _____

For _____

_____

Signed _____

Date _____

**Congratulations on graduating from Pre-Kindergarten!
You've worked so hard and have done a great job!**

_____

Name

_____

Teacher

_____

Date

No Child Left Behind

Teacher Jeanette is an initiative that emphasized the academic development of young children by making available books and workbooks that help parents and teachers inspire literacy and learning for children in African developing countries. We publish academic books students can relate to culturally.

We help to meet the basic needs of primary education for children living in an orphanage and rural communities. It is our goal to provide updated education to children without access to quality education. Visit our website for more information — www.liberialiterarysociety.org

Kinder Kollege Curriculum Details

Our Kinder Kollege 2-year curriculum, is suggested for a Teacher-to-student ratio of 1 teacher to 25 students and includes nine Teacher Jeanette Kinder Kollege workbooks (math, science, social studies, Bible stories, language arts, reading, writing, spelling, technology, and handwriting), and a backpack with school supplies.

L. M. Logan | Patrice Juah | Ophelia S. Lewis

216

Kinder Kollege Workbooks
Pre-K to Kindergarten

KINDER KOLLEGE
Language Arts Spelling

Pre-K
AND
KINDERGARTEN

OVER 200 SPELLING WORDS

Pyramid Words
Backwards Spelling
My Sentences
Upper and Lower Case
1, 2, & 3 Syllables
Word Search
Rhyming Words
Alphabetical Order
Spelling Lists: 1 to 9-Letter Words

L. M. Logan
Patrice Juah
Ophelia S. Lewis

Cover illustration by Shabamukama Osbert

KINDER KOLLEGE
Language Arts Reading

STRATEGIES & COMPREHENSION

Listening Speaking Viewing
Phonics and Fluency
Concepts About Print
Syllables in Spoken Words
Reading & Retelling Stories

Pre-K
and
Kindergarten

L. M. Logan
Patrice Juah
Ophelia S. Lewis

Cover illustration by Shabamukama Osbert

KINDER KOLLEGE
Language Arts
Writing

PRIMARY WRITING

Learn to Letter
Writing Fundamentals
Primary Composition
Handwriting Pratice
Persuasive Writing
Accessing Information

L. M. Logan
Patrice Juah
Ophelia S. Lewis

Cover illustration by Shabamukama Osbert

KINDER KOLLEGE
Math
Primary Arithmetic

Pre-K
and
Kindergarten

Numbers & Operations
Counting 1-100
Measurement
Shapes
Data Analysis

L. M. Logan
Patrice Juah
Ophelia S. Lewis

Cover illustration by Shabamukama Osbert

KINDER KOLLEGE
Primary Bible Lessons

L. M. Logan
Patrice Juah
Ophelia S. Lewis

Cover illustration by Shabamukama Osbert

KINDER KOLLEGE
Primary Copybook

Handwriting
Activities

Pre-K
and
Kindergarten

SUCCESS AT WRITING

Age appropriate line width

Bold lines for accurate
letter placement

Lots of Activities & Coloring

L. M. Logan
Patrice Juah
Ophelia S. Lewis

Cover illustration by Shabamukama Osbert

KINDER KOLLEGE
Science Smart Start

Science * Earth Science * Physical Science
Life Science * Plants & Animals
Healthy Habits * Our Body * Our Five Senses

L. M. Logan
Patrice Juah
Ophelia S. Lewis

Pre-K
and
Kindergarten

Cover illustration by Shabamukama Osbert

KINDER KOLLEGE
Social Studies
Liberia

VOTE
BALLOT

OUR NATION
Map and Globe
Good Citizenship
Community Helpers
Where We Live
Personal Finance
My Vote

L. M. Logan
Patrice Juah
Ophelia S. Lewis

Cover illustration by Shabamukama Osbert

KINDER KOLLEGE
Technology
Computer & Devices

USING TECHNOLOGY
IN SOLVING PROBLEMS

L. M. Logan
Patrice Juah
Ophelia S. Lewis

Cover illustration by Shabamukama Osbert

Teacher Jeanette Workbooks and Other Children's Books

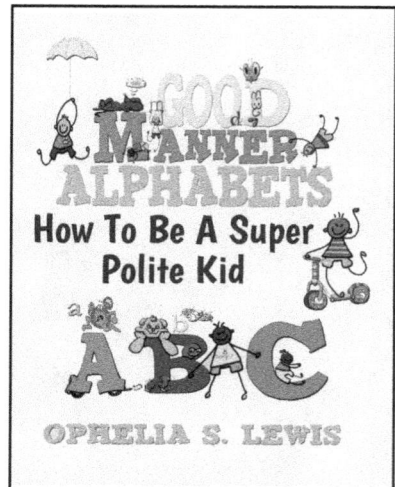

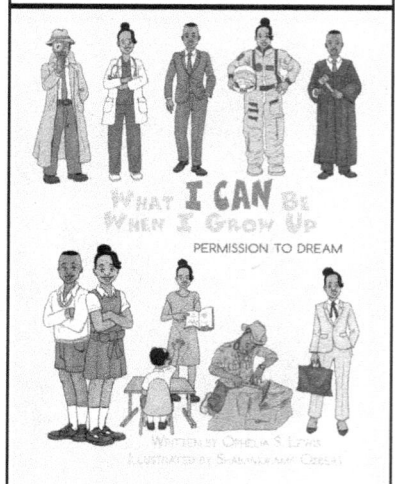

www.ingramcontent.com/pod-product-compliance
Lightning Source LLC
Chambersburg PA
CBHW081148090426
42736CB00017B/3232